JACOB K. JAVITS
R UNITED STATES SENATOR
NEW YORK

LES J. HITCH
DENT
ERSITY OF CALIFORNIA

UR F. BURNS
RMAN
IONAL BUREAU OF ECONOMIC RESEARCH

The D

HON.

SENIO

FROM

CHARL

PRES

UNIVE

ARTH

CHA

NAT

THE CHARLES C. M

The Defense Sector
and
the American Economy

THE CHARLES C. MOSKOWITZ LECTURES
SCHOOL OF COMMERCE
NEW YORK UNIVERSITY

NEW YORK   New York University Press

1968

LONDON   University of London Press Ltd.

© 1968 by New York University
Library of Congress Catalog Card Number 68–22812
Manufactured in the United States of America

ON JANUARY 17, 1961, President Eisenhower addressed a farewell message to the nation. His topic was "Liberty is at Stake," and he cautioned his fellow Americans to beware twin dangers to freedom from what he called the "military-industrial complex" and the "scientific-technological elite." His words were:

> . . . this conjunction of an immense military establishment and a large arms industry is new in the American experience. The total influence—economic, political, even spiritual—is felt in every city, every state house, every office of the Federal Government. We recognize the imperative need for this development. Yet we must not fail to comprehend its grave implications. Our toil, resources and livelihood are all involved; so is the very structure of our society.

In the councils of Government, we must guard
against the acquisition of unwarranted influence,
whether sought or unsought, by the military-industrial complex. The potential for the disastrous rise
of misplaced power exists and will persist.

We must never let the weight of this combination
endanger our liberties or democratic processes. We
should take nothing for granted. Only an alert and
knowledgeable citizenry can compel the proper
meshing of the huge industrial and military machinery of defense with our peaceful methods and
goals, so that security and liberty may prosper together.

Akin to, and largely responsible for the sweeping
changes in our industrial-military posture has been
the technological revolution during recent decades.
• • •
The prospect of domination of the nation's scholars
by Federal employment, project allocations and the
power of money is ever present, and is gravely to
be regarded.

Yet, in holding scientific research and discovery in
respect, as we should, we must also be alert to the
equal and opposite danger that public policy could
itself become the captive of a scientific-technological elite.*

It seems somewhat odd, but in the half-dozen years
since President Eisenhower's farewell address, his point
has generated very little public discussion. Is this because the danger is not real; or is real, but not perceived
as such by the public; or is real and so perceived, but
there is apathy? Given the vigor of the current debate

* See Appendix for the complete text of President Eisenhower's
address.

vis-à-vis the Vietnam conflict, the last possibility seems neither reasonable nor likely. While many words might be descriptive of the United States today, apathetic is surely not among them.

What, then, can be said about the military-industrial complex?

The question seemed so important and timely to many of us at the School of Commerce that we decided to devote the 1967 Moskowitz Lecture Series to the overall topic "The Defense Sector and the American Economy." The Moskowitz Lectures, established through the generosity of Charles C. Moskowitz, a distinguished alumnus of the School of Commerce and formerly Vice President, Treasurer, and a Director of Loew's, Inc., have enabled the School to make a significant contribution to public discussion and understanding of important issues affecting the American economy and its business enterprises.

Three outstanding Americans, men of extraordinary experience, insight, and intellect, were invited to articulate their thoughts on various aspects of the overall theme. Jacob K. Javits, senior United States Senator from the State of New York, chose to speak on "ABM: The Dynamics of a National Decision." Charles J. Hitch, now President of the University of California and a former Assistant Secretary of Defense, was invited to talk on "The Defense Sector: Its Impact on American Business." Arthur F. Burns, President of the National Bureau of Economic Research and Chairman of the Council of Economic Advisers under President Eisenhower, was asked to address the final audience on "The

Defense Sector: An Evaluation of Its Economic and
Social Impact."

Senator Javits used the decision recently announced
by Secretary of Defense McNamara, to deploy a thin
anti-ballistic missile defense against a potential Chinese
nuclear threat, to analyze the importance of President
Eisenhower's warning. In so doing, he directed specific
and emphatic comment to the "scientific-technological
elite," and expressed more concern over the danger of
this group's influence on basic national policy decisions
than he did over what he termed the "narrow world
of defense contractor lobbyists." Thus, Senator Javits
was deeply concerned over the efforts of many professional military men and important scientists who work
on military research, like Dr. Harold M. Agnew, head
of the Weapons Division of the AEC's Los Alamos
Scientific Laboratory, to get the United States to under-
take the building of a massive anti-ballistic missile system. These efforts are a particular source of worry to
the senator because he discerns beneath them the profoundly dangerous assumption by the scientists and technicians that their technical knowledge carries over into
the field of national policy. But policy is much broader,
for it involves the cultural and social values of the nation, and, consequently, how the country wishes to order
its priorities and allocate its resources and energies. In
such matters, the scientists and technicians are not necessarily more knowledgeable than others, and may, indeed, be less so than politicians or the public.

Mr. Hitch agreed with President Eisenhower's ob-
servation that the development of a defense sector in

the American economy is historically important and poses significant problems of analysis and policy for the nation. However, he did not share, at least to the same degree, the latter's concern over a monolithic military-industrial complex. Instead, Mr. Hitch perceived many relatively small and competitive military-industrial complexes, each pushing for its weapons system, branch of the service, firm, etc. In any case, he expressed the belief that continued adherence to our nation's tradition of civilian control over the military, plus a policy preventing employment of former Department of Defense and military personnel by firms over which they had power of decision in procurement (which policy would have to be adopted), would protect us from any major evils arising out of the "military-industrial complex."

Mr. Hitch noted that analysis of the impact of the defense sector on business was complicated by the inadequacy of statistical material, reflecting, in part, the fact that the defense sector is not well defined in statistical classifications. Despite this difficulty, the lecturer presented a careful analysis of the defense sector's impact on American business, both present and prospective. As background for the major present impacts, it was observed that in the decade of the 50's and in the early 60's, the major emphasis in the mix of defense spending was on missiles, aerospace, and electronics, but the Vietnam buildup had brought the conventional weaponry of limited warfare more prominently into the foreground. Mr. Hitch noted these major current impacts: (1) by industry, defense spending is mainly on ordnance (including missiles), aircraft, radio-TV, communications, and electronic components, except that service industries (e.g., warehousing, transportation) share significantly in employment generated by total defense spending (26 per cent), but are not much dependent on such spending for employment (defense-generated employment amounts to only 3 per cent of employment in the services category); (2) by business firm, defense spending is mainly with a relatively small number of very large firms, although some of these very large firms, like GM, are only little dependent on defense sales in relation to their total sales; (3) by region, defense spending is concentrated, both in terms of prime contracts and subcontracts, with California and New York the dominant states; and (4) by occupation, defense spending increases the employment of technical, scientific, and managerial manpower and reduces relatively that of production workers.

Two other important impacts were noted. In connection with Research and Development, Mr. Hitch observed that most basic research spending was not by private industry in the United States, but rather by the Department of Defense, NASA, and AEC, which jointly finance about two-thirds of all R and D. However, the militarily induced R and D has important spillover effects in the nondefense segments of the economy. The speaker observed also that the change in 1961 from a cost-plus-fixed-fee procurement pricing policy to a firm fixed price or incentive contract arrangement, with the widest possible competition, had resulted in vastly improved efficiency—an impact of benefit to business, government, and the public.

Looking to the future, and assuming no unpredictable technological breakthroughs and no basic change in the state of the world, Mr. Hitch expected a shift in the mix of defense spending back toward somewhat greater emphasis on strategic retaliatory forces (development of multiple nuclear warheads) and on intercontinental defense forces (development of the "thin" ABM system, and some subsequent "thickening" which the speaker considered likely). Of course, the foregoing shift would be expansive for the missile, aircraft, electronics, and communications industries, as it would be for Research and Development and for employment of technical, scientific, and managerial manpower. However, spending on conventional weaponry would, assuming no further limited wars and a conclusion to the Vietnam war, fall to a lower level and plateau at a point sufficient to maintain an immediately available general purpose force. Mr. Hitch expected concentration of defense spending by firm and by geographical area to continue.

Mr. Hitch concluded by commenting on two frequently discussed matters: (1) the impact on business of a drastic cutback in defense spending; and (2) the procurement pricing policy adopted in 1961. He expressed little concern over the former, noting that the nation had weathered well the cutbacks after World War II and Korea, and adding that diversification of defense-oriented industries and firms was a feasible and desirable development. With respect to the latter, he favored continuation of the "efficiency" criterion adopted in 1961, and opposed the suggestion that "fair share" or "social cost" criteria should be applied in procurement by the defense sector. He favored specific, direct, and identified programs for the improvement of depressed areas and industries, rather than the indirect pursuit of such ends through defense procurement policy.

Dr. Burns did not seem to discern, any more than the prior lecturers, any danger to America from a conspiratorial and monolithic military-industrial complex. However, viewing the military-industrial complex as being the same as the defense sector, he perceived a number of important economic, social, and political impacts.

From the economic side, Dr. Burns observed that huge defense expenditures, superimposed on rising non-defense governmental outlays due to urban and other problems, had pushed government spending to enormous levels, and, consequently, revolutionized government finances in our generation. Thus, great expenditures have meant very high taxes, the creation of serious inflationary pressures (for the price level surges upward when defense expenditures rise sharply), and the deterioration of our balance of payments position. The last named consequence adversely affects foreign confidence in the dollar and America's future political position in the world.

Also from the economic side, the growth of the defense sector has involved the real cost of drawing productive resources away from the production of non-defense goods and services, which are consequently foregone. Thus, although Dr. Burns recognizes that the times are dangerous and large defense expenditures are unavoidable, he adds, ". . . if the resources devoted to military and space activities during the past decade had been put instead to civilian uses, we could surely have eliminated urban slums, besides adding liberally to private investment in new plant and equipment as well as to both public and private investment in human capital." Significantly, Dr. Burns drew the attention of his listeners to the millions of workers employed in defense-related production, adding the point that the defense sector employs a larger proportion of skilled and high-brainpower persons than would be found in the non-defense sectors of the economy.

From the social side, Dr. Burns observed several serious impacts of the defense sector. He thought that the restlessness of contemporary youth was one, and pointed out that the institutionalization of compulsory military service upsets the lives of young people in a variety of disturbing ways. He expressed concern also over the impact of the defense sector on our educational system, noting that: (1) the defense sector emphasizes science, mathematics, and foreign languages, in addition to encouraging research activity, with consequent de-emphasis on the humanities and philosophy, as well as teaching; and (2) the defense sector introduces elements of secrecy into university research activity, and tends to inhibit open criticism of the government by university administrators and professors who are benefitting from government grants.

Of course, the last point has a political side. With respect to politics, Dr. Burns observed that the huge size of military budgets and the incomplete disclosure concerning their management involved the danger of political abuse, for defense expenditures could be used to achieve other than national security objectives. His concern here was directed more to a potential danger than to an actual, present one. And he worried about the inherent danger to individual freedom which great government growth carries, especially when that growth is induced by national security considerations.

In concluding, Dr. Burns saw the defense sector continuing as a formidable factor in America's economic, social, and political life. Much more, he saw it generating political divisiveness and tension in our nation. Thus, he perceived two conflicting schools of thought. The first school is worried mainly about an external Communist threat, seen as a centrally-directed conspiracy. This school is anxious to give priority in our allocation of resources to the creation of enormous military power, which can defeat or at least withstand that threat. The second school is worried mainly about internal threats to the nation, originating in the deterioration of our cities and the needs of Negroes and other minority groups for immediate large-scale improvement. This school sees the Communist countries split by nationalistic rivalries, and is consequently unready and unwilling to give high priority to the creation of military power. Although economic growth makes possible both more guns and more butter, neither group is satisfied to advance toward its goal at the pace of normal economic growth. Of course, the outcome of the conflict of national goals and priorities is profoundly important. Without wanting us to strip ourselves of our capacity for defense, Dr. Burns expressed the belief "that our national security depends not only on awesome military forces, but also on the strength of our economic system and the wholesomeness of our social and political life." And so he hoped that we, as well as the peoples of the Communist countries, would "bring the mad armaments race under decent control."

The foregoing review of the 1967 Moskowitz Lectures indicates the answer to the major question posed earlier: Is the relative lack of public discussion of the danger which President Eisenhower warned against in his farewell address a reflection of its not being real, or of a lack of public perception or apathy? None of the speakers perceived danger from a conspiratorial or monolithic military-industrial complex, although Senator Javits expressed worry about the "scientific-technological elite." Indeed, he used the decision to deploy a "thin" ABM system as a vehicle for conveying his concern. Both Mr. Hitch and Dr. Burns appeared more impressed with the magnitude of the defense sector and its undesigned and unintended, but vitally important impacts— some good, but many not so good—on all aspects of American life: business, education, politics, moral values, psychological sense of well- or ill-being, economic and social progress, status in the world, and so on, and on, and on. Thus, if we view the "military-industrial complex" as no more than the defense sector, then we need have no present fear of an evil conspiracy, but we should have real and continuing concern over the substantial and negative impacts. And, by drawing our attention to these, this year's Moskowitz Lecturers have clarified and amplified the significance of President Eisenhower's warning.

Finally, it would be ungracious if I did not express again the sincerely felt gratitude of the School of Commerce, as well as mine, to our friend, Mr. Charles C. Moskowitz, whose continued support makes these lectures possible, and to our lecturers, Senator Javits, Mr. Hitch, and Dr. Burns. All three gave extensively of their wide and deep perception of the problem before us. My thanks go also to my administrative assistant, Miss Olga Budor, whose many hours were devoted to achieving a smoothly-run program and whose editorial skills brought these papers to publication.

Abraham L. Gitlow,
DEAN
SCHOOL OF COMMERCE
NEW YORK UNIVERSITY

January 1968

THE CHARLES C. MOSKOWITZ LECTURES

THE MOSKOWITZ LECTURES have been established through the generosity of a distinguished alumnus of the School of Commerce, Mr. Charles C. Moskowitz of the Class of 1914, who retired after many years as Vice President-Treasurer and a Director of Loew's, Inc.

In establishing these lectures it was Mr. Moskowitz' aim to contribute to an understanding of the function of business and its underlying disciplines in society by providing a public forum for the dissemination of enlightened business theories and practices.

The School of Commerce and New York University are deeply grateful to Mr. Moskowitz for his continued interest in and contribution to the educational and public service program of his Alma Mater.

This volume is the eighth in the Moskowitz series. The earlier ones were:

February 1961   *Business Survival in the Sixties*
THOMAS F. PATTON, President and
Chief Executive Officer
Republic Steel Corporation

November 1961   *The Challenges Facing*
Management
DON G. MITCHELL, President
General Telephone and Electronics
Corporation

November 1962   *Competitive Private Enterprise*
Under Government Regulation
MALCOLM A. McINTYRE, President
Eastern Air Lines

November 1963   *The Common Market: Friend or*
Competitor?
JESSE W. MARKHAM, Professor of
Economics, Princeton University
CHARLES E. FIERO, Vice President
The Chase Manhattan Bank
HOWARD S. PIQUET, Senior Specialist
in International Economics,
Legislative Reference Service,
The Library of Congress

November 1964   *The Forces Influencing the*
American Economy
JULES BACKMAN, Research Professor
of Economics,
New York University
MARTIN R. GAINSBRUGH,
Chief Economist and Vice President,
National Industrial Conference
Board

CONTENTS

ABM: THE DYNAMICS OF A NATIONAL DECISION

by Senator Jacob K. Javits

ON SEPTEMBER 18, in a truly remarkable speech, Defense Secretary McNamara announced the Administration's decision to deploy a "thin" anti-ballistic missile defense against a potential threat from Communist China. This decision was one of the most complex, and portentous in its ramifications, of any that has been made in the past decade. The decision has implications which impinge, directly or indirectly, on every important aspect of our national life. A study of the dynamics of this decision is very instructive.

First I wish to comment on what I consider to be the inadequacy of the national debate which preceded the ABM decision. Ostensibly, one might attribute the inadequacies of the debate to the complexity of the technical considerations involved in an anti-ballistic missile system. There is no doubt that most Americans are intimidated by the language of science and technology.

However, as I followed, and later reviewed the ABM debate, I was struck by the fact that there was relatively little dispute over purely technical questions. By contrast, however, there was very earnest dispute over a wide spectrum of the most fundamental policy considerations which were involved in the ABM decision.

While pressures were exerted from many quarters during the ABM debate, it is clear that the decision-making process was throughout dominated by Secretary McNamara. Indeed, we owe him a debt of national gratitude for having forced a shift in the focus of the ABM debate away from essentially technical considerations and for having forcefully brought to public attention the fundamental policy considerations involved in the ABM decision.

There were pressures from many quarters during the ABM debate. One might assume that many of these pressures came from what is called the "military-industrial complex." After all, there are, potentially at least, tens of billions of dollars worth of contracts involved in building an ABM system. However, I have not discovered any discernible efforts by the great defense contracting corporations to influence the ABM debate or its outcome. This is not always true of national debates and decisions on defense questions, as you all know.

Having made that statement, I wish to modify it in one respect. It was President Eisenhower, in his farewell address to the nation, who brought to public attention the dangers posed by the "military-industrial complex." As President Eisenhower used the term, he was talking about something much more expansive and ramified than the narrow world of defense-contractor lobbyists who abound in Washington and who have come to be thought of in the public mind as being the "military-industrial complex."

In the wider sense that President Eisenhower used the phrase—to include entrenched elements in the military establishment itself and in its vast dependent intellectual establishment sustained by government contract—the "military-industrial complex" was active in the ABM debate and did seek manfully to determine its outcome. There is nothing improper about this. In fact, that is just the plain duty of the Joint Chiefs of Staff.

I spoke earlier of the technical complexity of an ABM system, and of how this tends to inhibit participation in debate by those who do not have a technical background. I think that this is a very real danger.

In his farewell address President Eisenhower also warned of the ". . . danger that public policy could itself become the captive of a scientific-technological elite." Largely because of Secretary McNamara's alertness and zeal, this did not happen in the present case of the ABM decision. The danger was definitely present, however, and will be present again in future decisions on the ABM system. I will give you a very graphic example.

Dr. Harold M. Agnew, head of the Weapons Division of the AEC's Los Alamos Scientific Laboratory, made a speech to the Air Force Association on March 16, in San Francisco. Dr. Agnew's speech is an open attack on Secretary McNamara's general conduct and specifically of his views on the ABM question. It is a pure example of the expression of the view of the "scientific-technological elite" which President Eisenhower warned us of, and I commend to you a study of its full text. For illustrative purposes, I will just quote one sentence. After taking Secretary McNamara to task for his entire strategic philosophy and his opposition to a Soviet-oriented ABM system, Dr. Agnew says:

> I believe the lack of true understanding of science and technology of many of our policy makers, and what I consider the substitution of wishful thinking, is very dangerous, and could become more and more serious.

In my judgment Dr. Agnew's knowledge of science and technology is most useful and essential to us. The problem is the tendency of this elite to get out of their field, to think they have equal expertise and authority on broad matters of public policy. And most troublesome are their recurring efforts to have basic policy questions decided on the basis of technological factors on which they are expert but which are inadequate criteria for judging basic questions of national goals and values.

I would like to turn now to some of the differences between Secretary McNamara and the Joint Chiefs of Staff which emerged in the course of the ABM debate. The Joint Chiefs understood their role in this debate. But a close study of the record shows that some fundamental differences exist between the Secretary of Defense and the Joint Chiefs of Staff with regard to our relationship to the Soviet Union. Secretary McNamara believes that it is both possible and essential to achieve an understanding with the Soviets to stabilize the "balance of terror" which keeps the peace. He is passionately concerned over avoiding a new round of the arms race and believes that accurate communication of intention is a crucial factor. I quote a brief passage of his San Francisco speech as an example:

> . . . they could not read our intentions with any greater accuracy than we could read theirs. And thus the result has been that we have both built up our forces to a point that far exceeds a credible second-strike capability against the forces we each started with.

The alternative which he poses to an understanding on strategic weapons is:

> . . . both the Soviets and ourselves would be forced to continue on a foolish and feckless course. . . . The time has come for us both to realize that, and to act reasonably. It is clearly in our mutual interest to do so.

The approach of the Joint Chiefs is quite different. Their view, as reflected in General Wheeler's statement to Congress, is based on the traditional concept of an adversary relationship with the Soviet Union and contrasts sharply with the innovative thinking of McNamara. An illustrative example is the following quote from General Wheeler's statement:

> We do not pretend to be able to predict with certainty just how the Soviets will react. We do know from experience the high price they must pay to overcome a deployed U.S. ABM system.

The record also shows that the civilian Defense Secretary and the uniformed Joint Chiefs have very different assessments of the diplomatic leverage provided by nuclear weapons. Secretary McNamara says:

> Unlike any other era in military history, today a substantial numerical superiority of weapons does not effectively translate into political control, or diplomatic leverage.

General Wheeler has a quite different view.

> . . . at the time of Cuba, the strategic nuclear balance was such that the Soviets did not have an exploitable capability, because of our vastly superior nuclear strength. And to bring this forward into the present context, it's also the view of the Joint Chiefs that regardless of anyone's views about the situation in Vietnam, we think it quite clear that we would have had even more hesitation in deploying our forces there, had the strategic nuclear balance not been in our favor.

I think it would be instructive at this point to juxtapose another set of quotes. The question at issue involves judgments as to the allocation of resources. While the initial cost of our "thin" ABM defense will be around $4 billion, it is common knowledge that further refinements could lead to expenditures of at least $40 to $50 billion for a "heavy" defense system. Secretary Mc-Namara's view is succinct:

> I know of nothing we could do today that would waste more of our resources or add more to our risks.

By way of contrast, the Chairman of the House Armed Services Committee expressed the following view.

We are an affluent nation . . . we are now right at $750 billion GNP; and responsible people tell us it is headed for a trillion. So we can afford it. Why not have the two of them, and keep the Soviets off balance . . . ?

The most shockingly neglected aspect of the ABM debate has been what is ultimately the basic issue—the allocation of national resources. The magnitude of potential costs is very great—$50 billion, and a lot more if a civilian fallout shelter program were added on. Expenditures of this order of magnitude could have profound warping effects on the total pattern of our national life. It is essential that public men, both in and out of government, join the continuing debate over the need and justification for an anti-ballistic missile defense. Now is the time when we need the views and judgments of our nation's best minds. Later, when we might be irrevocably tied to the ABM roller coaster, their post-mortem dissent will be of little value.

If there is any lesson we should have learned from our Vietnam experience, it is the danger of not taking a long look down the road ahead before we commit ourselves to something. In Vietnam, initial small expenditures and periodic increments that were modest at first have now snowballed into a $30 billion per year affair. We find ourselves faced with a high cost in human life and misery and inflationary threats, while our urgent urban needs are not adequately met. The lessons of Vietnam in this regard are applicable to the ABM debate, and I repeat my earnest exhortation that this whole matter be given the closest scrutiny *now* by the men whose views are respected in all areas of national endeavor.

Decisions regarding national security are perhaps the most difficult of all decisions. We live in a very complicated and dangerous world. An atmosphere of insecurity prevails everywhere. But there is no such thing as absolute security, and security certainly is not solely or even primarily a question of weapons systems. Maximum security is derived from the optimum balance and quality of national life. Secretary McNamara had some pertinent things to say in this regard in a speech he gave in Montreal in May of 1966:

> A nation can reach the point at which it does not buy more security for itself simply by buying more military hardware—we are at that point. The decisive factor for a powerful nation—already adequately armed—is the character of its relationships with the world.

At this point I cannot resist quoting the opposing view of Dr. Agnew, the Los Alamos Weapons Division chief:

> I would argue that there are few nations whom we should worry about as far as world opinion is concerned. These are only the nations with whom we are engaged in competition and who may have the military and economic strength to materially affect what we are doing.

I think the important point is that all of us have a real competence and a real contribution to make when the broad questions of national security are involved. The weapons cultists notwithstanding, the quality of our schools, the physical and mental health of our population, the social justice barometers of our big cities—are all factors which determine our national security.

While most of the ABM debate has been concerned with our relations with the Soviet Union, the ABM system finally decided on is oriented against Communist China. In his San Francisco speech McNamara said there were "marginal grounds" for concluding that the deployment of a China-oriented system would be "prudent."

This is neither a very enthusiastic nor a very convincing line of argument and the suspicion persists that the decision to proceed with a "thin" ABM deployment was attributable in fact to considerations other than Peking's nuclear capability and potential. James Reston of *The New York Times* has dubbed the ABM "the anti-Republican Missile." I will not deny that there has been a partisan dimension to this entire issue with both Democrats and Republicans maneuvering for party advantage in a preelection year, and Mr. Reston may well be correct when he accuses the President of ". . . not dealing with the problems before him but with the politics of the problems" in making his ABM decision. In any event, it is most unfortunate that we have not heard the President's views of the very fundamental substantive considerations involved in the ABM controversy.

However, this line of inquiry does not lead us very far. Let us turn instead to the rationale which is now being expounded with regard to Communist China as a reason why we need a $5 billion "thin" ABM defense.

In a major follow-up speech on October 6, Assistant Defense Secretary Warnke addressed himself to this and other issues not gone into by Secretary McNamara in his earlier San Francisco speech.

Among other things, Mr. Warnke argues that our anti-China ABM will reinforce President Johnson's 1963 pledge to protect non-nuclear states against Chinese nuclear blackmail and thus make it easier for Asian nations to sign the Non-Proliferation Treaty. Mr. Warnke's reasoning is ingenious but dubious in its accuracy. For instance, on October 1, an Indian Foreign Ministry publication had the following to say:

> The Government of India's decision not to sign the Nuclear Non-Proliferation Treaty stands intact in spite of big power pressure. The question of guarantees by the United States and the Soviet Union either jointly or individually has been dismissed as unworkable.

There are several passages in Mr. Warnke's remarks concerning Communist China which merit close attention because of their wider implications for U.S. policy. Parenthetically, it is most unfortunate that Secretary Rusk, who has recently conjured up the frightening image of "a billion Chinese on the Mainland, armed with nuclear weapons," has not given us his views of Mr. Warnke's assessment which follows:

We see no reason to conclude that the Chinese are any less cautious than the rulers of other nations that have nuclear weapons. . . . Indeed the Chinese have shown a disposition to act cautiously, and to avoid any military clash with the United States that could lead to nuclear war.

Following on the heels of this most interesting assessment of Peking's policy-orientation, Mr. Warnke goes on to state:

In deploying this system, we seek to emphasize the present unique disparity in strategic nuclear capability between the U.S. and China and to extend well into the future the credibility of our option for a nuclear response.

He also affirms that our ABM deployment will end:

. . . any uncertainty as to whether or not the United States would act to prevent the Chinese from gaining any political or military advantage from their nuclear forces.

Implicit in Mr. Warnke's exposition of policy is an apparent assumption that the Soviet Union would not honor its defense treaty commitments to Peking in the event of a U.S. nuclear strike at the Mainland. I think this point requires a definite clarification and I intend to seek one from both Secretary Rusk and Secretary McNamara.

Administration spokesmen have been largely silent on the impact of the ABM decision on our relations with our NATO allies, and there is evidence that this very important aspect of the decision was not given sufficient consideration.

According to press reports, our ABM decision has been received with skepticism and disfavor in most NATO capitals. Two of our closest Allies, Canada and the U.K., have publicly deplored the McNamara announcement. At a minimum, NATO feathers were unnecessarily ruffled by a lack of consultation on an important issue, at a time when the whole Alliance is passing through an internal crisis of confidence. According to a Washington *Post* survey the only NATO capital that took heart from our ABM decision was Paris, and that for reasons which are not necessarily helpful to our national interests. The *Post* reports that the French are having a "field day" with the "disquiet caused by the American decision" and see it as "a new vindication for their policy of disengagement from the Atlantic Alliance."

It is not my intention tonight to offer definitive answers to the many profound questions which have been raised in the course of this review of the dynamics of an important national decision. Rather, I have tried to suggest the scope and the implications of the issues which are involved. There are others too which I have not even sketched in this brief *tour d'horizon*. If it does accomplish anything, I think this review dramatizes the inadequacy of the national debate of the ramifications of opting for an anti-ballistic missile defense. It is clear, however, that only the initial round of debate has been concluded. The proponents of a full-blown "heavy" ABM defense against the Soviet Union have been denied victory on this round by Secretary McNamara's adamacy and by his compromise action in agreeing to a "thin" anti-Chinese ABM deployment. But we are now experiencing but a brief hiatus before the battle is renewed.

It is imperative therefore that the full weight of all elements and all points of view in our society be mobilized to participate proportionately in the next round of debate. It is only in this way that we can be assured of a truly national decision which reflects the true balance of our national interests.

The basic issues have now surfaced. They need further clarification and refinement, and much more searching exploration. As one Senator, I shall do my utmost to assure that we have a real national debate before we move any further down the road to a Buck Rogers world of missiles and counter missiles where fatalities are counted in the "megadeaths." Concurrently, I shall do my utmost to insure that the proper issues are debated and that decisions are not camouflaged by illusory technical jargon intended to intimidate or exclude the layman from the decision making process. It is in this aspect of the challenge that our universities can play their most vital role. I entreat you to join in this defense of the national interest.

THE DEFENSE SECTOR:
ITS IMPACT ON AMERICAN BUSINESS

by Charles J. Hitch

FOUR CHARACTERISTICS combine to give today's defense sector an impact upon American business which is unique in the history of our nation. These characteristics are the substantially high level of defense spending, its continuing nature, the growth of defense industries, and the constant push to extend the frontiers of military technology. Operating together, these factors have given much of American business a new and different look since the early 1950's.

HISTORICAL CHANGES

Present United States expenditures for national defense (including military assistance, AEC, and NASA) constitute approximately 10 per cent of our gross national product. This figure is, of course, far lower than peak wartime rates—during World War II the proportion soared to about 40 per cent. But the present 10 per cent is considerably above the levels of approximately 4 to 5 per cent in the years immediately following World War II. More important, defense spending has continued at a relatively high level for a decade and a half and shows no likelihood of significant reduction in the foreseeable future. Thus defense income has become a substantial and more-or-less normal factor in the economic reckoning of many American businesses.

The economic scene of the past few years is distinguished also by the emergence of a new phenomenon, the defense industry. Prior to World War II, defense industries as such were virtually nonexistent. American business directed its productive capacity almost exclusively to civilian markets in time of peace. When the nation found itself at war, business converted as quickly as possible to production of the tools of war. And when war ended, it reconverted as quickly to its normal civilian products. Today there are many industries whose defense production constitutes a relatively minor part of their operations, and whose defense products are closely related to their civilian products. But there are other industries, and a number of individual firms, whose major production effort is specifically directed to defense items and whose products bear little or no resemblance to those in the civilian sector.

These defense industries grow out of the increasing gap between civilian and military technology, the growing specialization and sophistication of the tools of war, and the pressure to extend the state of the art as a major means of maintaining military ascendancy.

Throughout most of our history as a nation, military technology was sufficiently similar to civilian technology so that conversion from one to the other presented few problems. The gunsmiths who made the muskets for the hunting and household protection needs of the early settlers could turn out arms for military use during colonial times. Powder manufacturers who were making blasting powder for the westward expansion of the railroads could produce gunpowder for Civil War armament. The First World War found some industries momentarily adapting their normal civilian products to military needs. When the Germans surrendered, these industries returned to the output of peacetime products. This same pattern—temporary conversion to military output, with innovation in weaponry dependent primarily on advances in civilian technology—continued well into World War II. The one exception was shipbuilding, where the development of armor plate, naval gunnery, the submarine, and the torpedo gave rise to what could truly be called a specialized defense industry.

World War II saw the first extensive effort to extend military technology well beyond the levels achieved in peacetime industrial production. The conscious scientific effort to develop new military tools resulted in rapid achievements in electronics and rocketry, and culminated in the development of the atom bomb.

Scientific work in military technology and in the military and civilian uses of atomic energy continued after World War II, but on a relatively small scale. It took the growing tensions of the Cold War and the outbreak of Korean hostilities to push new developments in military technology and to translate them into operational readiness. Increasingly, these developments led in directions totally different from civilian technology and markets. In other countries where similar advances in military technology were also taking place, the governments assumed much of the responsibility for both design and production. The United States, however, is unique in the degree to which we rely upon private enterprise for the provision of defense materiel, and for defense research and development as well. Accordingly, new firms quickly sprang into existence and some totally new industries evolved to produce the specialized innovations of the new military technology.

I shall not dwell on the underlying reasons for the high continuing levels and the directions of our defense spending. The two fundamental causes are obvious. The first, of course, is the current division of a substantial portion of the world between two basically opposing forces. In defense of our own nation and in support of our allies abroad, we must stand ready at all times to meet the military threat from Communist Russia in Europe and from Communist China in Asia. Russia is powerful now. China with its developing industrial base and its millions of people is steadily acquiring power. While we must hope that the military threat from these nations will eventually abate, we cannot realistically expect that to happen in the near future.

The second fundamental cause is the status of modern military technology. Weapons are now global in their reach, unprecedented in their destructiveness, and almost instant in their delivery. A nation under major attack no longer has the time to mobilize its industry, to convert its peacetime businesses to wartime production, to update its military technology. Its potential retaliatory time is cut to hours and even to minutes. On the other hand, tremendous lead-time is now required for development of the sophisticated weaponry of modern defense. Key weapon systems may take five, or ten, or even more years from initial design to construction of prototypes to actual production and deployment. This revolution in military technology is irreversible: never again can we resume our historical pattern of converting our factories to military production after the need arises. Defense thus appears destined to exert a significant and more or less permanent impact on American business, at least until the world turns a not-yet-foreseeable corner toward lasting peace.

THE NEED FOR BETTER DATA

The relative novelty of the American defense sector makes a review of its impact on business difficult at this time. One reason is that economists have not yet had, or taken, the time to study the subject in definitive detail. Another is that systematic and comparable data in the field are seriously lacking. As Jacoby and Stockfish point out, official economic statistics are based on a classification system that reflects the problems and concerns of an earlier day. "For this reason," they state, "there is no 'defense sector' now identified in official, standard industrial classifications. Yet one clearly exists, insofar as a substantial portion of the nation's economic activity and resources are devoted to performing a function that differs markedly from the functions of other resource-using activities." [1]

In the absence of systematic data, various government and private agencies and scholars have made studies of one or another aspect of the defense sector. Many of these differ in years covered, breakdowns by industry or by defense product, and definitions of defense spending—they may or may not include military assistance or AEC or NASA, or they may simply fail to specify precisely what is covered. The resulting data are generally noncomparable, and their use is highly frustrating to students of the economics of defense, or at least to one Moskowitz lecturer.

In 1963 President Johnson appointed a Committee on the Economic Impact of Defense and Disarmament. In his memorandum of appointment he said:

> The Committee will be responsible for the review and coordination of activities in the various departments and agencies designed to improve our understanding of the economic impact of defense expenditures and of changes either in the composition or in the total level of such expenditures.[2]

In its first report to the President in 1965, the Committee stated:

1 Neil H. Jacoby and J. A. Stockfish, "The Scope and Nature of the Defense Sector of the U.S. Economy," in *Planning and Forecasting in the Defense Industries,* ed. J. A. Stockfish (Belmont, California: Wadsworth Publishing Company, Inc., 1962), p. 2.

2 Memorandum of the President to the Hon. Robert S. McNamara *et al.*, December 21, 1963.

. . . there is vital need for more adequate, comprehensive, and accurate *information and analysis* of the impact of defense programs on the U.S. economy.[3]

The Committee cited a number of studies underway at various departments but warned that their completion "will still leave numerous gaps to be filled if the most intelligent choices of private and public policies are to be available."[4]

Among the major research programs undertaken after the Committee's establishment was the Economic Impact Project initiated by the Department of Defense in early 1964. Studies completed to date under that program have provided us with some of the best current data.

Using these and other available materials, I should like now to offer what must of necessity be a highly impressionistic view of various aspects of the defense impact on American business.

SHIFTS IN THE DEFENSE "MIX"

While the total level of defense spending as a percentage of national product has remained more or less stable for the past decade or so, broad shifts have occurred in the composition of the overall program. This shifting pattern will undoubtedly continue to be an important feature of the defense sector. The year-to-year

3 *Report of the Committee on the Economic Impact of Defense and Disarmament* (Washington, D.C.: U.S. Government Printing Office, July, 1965), p. 56.
4 *Ibid.*, p. 65.

allocation of the defense budget must respond to the constantly changing international situation, the Communist bloc's military innovations, and our own technological breakthroughs. Thus the late 1950's and early 1960's brought a heavy concentration on missiles and other items of the strategic retaliatory force buildup, reflecting both technological advances and the necessity to match Russian strategic strength and maintain the "balance of terror." Expenditures in this area leveled off as the major systems were brought to readiness in the early 1960's. Defense spending then began to show the effects of the growing Vietnam action. Impacts were shifting from aerospace and electronics and missile industries and toward the industries producing the more "conventional" weapons of limited war: field and hand weapons, planes and helicopters, tanks, uniforms, and the array of materiel needed to support troops in the field. A substantial portion of defense spending today is going to the producers of these defense requirements—producers that in many instances are not classified among the defense industries.

Meantime, a new round of strategic and global defense buildup appears to be underway, as indicated by recent announcements of plans for a thin anti-missile umbrella and for new multiple-warhead missiles. The anti-missile program responds to Communist China's developing nuclear and missile technology. The multiple-warhead missiles reflect a new technological breakthrough and a move to update the missile systems completed in the early 1960's.

THE MAJOR POINTS OF IMPACT

Each of these shifts changes the impact of defense spending on various industries, firms, and geographic regions. Let us now look at the impact in terms of these classifications.

The Industries Involved

Industrial involvement in the defense sector needs to be examined from two different viewpoints. The first is each industry's share of the total government outlay for defense spending. The second is the degree of each industry's reliance on defense income. Some large industries may rank very high in their share of total defense production and yet rank relatively low in their reliance on defense income—that is to say, they may ship a much smaller part of their total output to defense purchasers than to civilian purchasers. Other industries may rank lower in their share of total defense production and yet be very highly dependent on defense income, i.e., they ship most of their output to the government rather than to civilian purchasers. A few industries, notably aircraft, missiles, communications equipment, and shipbuilding and ordnance, rank high on both scales. These latter groups comprise the major "defense industries."

Industry Shares of Defense Activity

A general picture of the distribution of defense spending among American industries may be derived from a breakdown of the military prime contract procurement program. The most detailed study to date—available, unfortunately, only for fiscal year 1963—breaks down the entire military prime contract procurement program by the traditional industrial classification, the SIC Product Code, at the four-digit level.[5] The resulting table shows that the procurement program is spread over seventy-eight different industries, but that seven industrial categories account for more than three-fourths of the total military prime contracts. Three of those categories are concerned with aircraft (aircraft, aircraft engines and parts, other aircraft equipment), and they together account for 34 per cent of the entire procurement program. In second place is the "Radio, TV communication equipment" industry, with 20 per cent of the total. Shipbuilding and repairing ranks third, complete guided missiles fourth, and ammunition not elsewhere classified fifth.

A new study has just been published which uses 1967 figures and, more importantly, a much broader measure of defense spending impact, not restricted to prime contractors. Richard P. Oliver, in the September, 1967, issue of the *Monthly Labor Review*, reports the distribution of defense-generated employment among in-

5 Research Analysis Corporation, *Economic Impact Analysis: A Military Procurement Final-Demand Vector* (Study for Department of Defense, 1967, Vol. I), pp. 9–10, 15, 36.

dustries in 1967, as calculated by the processing of data
on military purchases through an interindustry model.[6]
The model, developed as part of the Interagency Growth
Project, estimates the direct and indirect effects of purchases, tracing chains of input requirements from prime
contractors back through the more basic stages of production, distribution, and transportation.

While most of the other available interindustry
data focus primarily on manufacturing, Oliver's information shows that 26 per cent of defense-generated
employment in 1967 actually fell in the category of
services, particularly transportation and warehousing,
with 7 per cent, and wholesale and retail trade, with 6
per cent. Sixty-eight per cent of defense-generated employment was in manufacturing, and here the leading
industries were aircraft and parts, with 16 per cent,
radio, television, and communications equipment, with
8 per cent, and ordnance (including missiles), with 6
per cent. No other industry exceeded 3 per cent. Oliver's
study helps to correct the tendency to overemphasize
the importance of the big weapons manufacturers and
to underrate the effects of defense spending on other
sectors of American business.

Industry Reliance on Defense Income

One measure of each industry's reliance on defense
income is its government shipments. Information on

6 Richard P. Oliver, "The Employment Effect of Defense Expenditures," *Monthly Labor Review* (September, 1967), pp.
9–16.

shipments was collected by the Bureau of the Census in 1963 and again in 1965 for six major "defense-oriented" industry groups, some of them covering as many as five SIC-coded individual industries at the four-digit level. These figures include major subcontracting. In 1963, 68 per cent of the total shipments for these six industry groups went to the government. By 1965 the total figure for the six groups had dropped substantially, to 54 per cent. The percentage of government shipments by individual groups differed considerably in each year, ranging from 80 per cent for aircraft and missile products to 9 per cent for machinery in 1965. All six industries showed a decline in percentage of government shipments from 1963 to 1965.[7]

These industry groups, except for shipbuilding, are heavily involved in procurement for strategic retaliatory forces, and the declines in the percentage of their shipments going to the government undoubtedly reflect the cutback in funds for strategic retaliatory forces between 1963 and 1965 as programs initiated earlier reached required levels of strength. They also reflect the beginning effects of the shift in defense allocations toward general purpose forces and general support in response to Vietnam hostilities, programs in which these industry groups play a less concentrated part.

Percentage changes in government shipments do not necessarily indicate absolute declines in either de-

7 *1963 Census of Manufacturers* and *Shipments of Defense-Oriented Industries 1965,* U.S. Department of Commerce, Bureau of the Census.

fense shipments or total shipments. Expanding civilian purchases may also account for percentage reductions in defense shipments. Actually, both causes were in operation in this instance: total defense shipments for the six groups declined somewhat while nondefense shipments rose substantially from 1963 to 1965.

The Oliver article mentioned earlier also reports defense-generated employment for each industry in 1967 as a percentage of the industry's total employment. The two industries most dependent on defense spending by this measure are ordnance (including missiles) and aircraft and parts. Also ranking high in defense dependence are radio, television, and communications equipment, electronic components and accessories, machine shop products, and "other transportation equipment" (including shipbuilding). Defense-generated employment as a percentage of total employment for these six groups ranges from 65 per cent for ordnance to 23 per cent for other transportation equipment. While the services account for 26 per cent of total defense employment, less than 3 per cent of employment in the services is defense-generated.[8]

The Firms Involved

Most of the important defense firms are big businesses, and some are among the biggest in the United States. A recent study prepared for the Department of Defense points out:

8 Richard P. Oliver, pp. 9–11.

Of the 100 largest defense prime contractors in fiscal year 1963, 39 were among the largest 100 U.S. industrial corporations, 2 were among the 50 largest U.S. utility companies, and 2 were among the 50 largest U.S. transportation companies. Sixty-nine of the largest 100 defense contractors were included among the largest 500 industrial corporations for 1963.[9]

The one hundred top companies in dollar volume of military prime contracts in fiscal year 1966 accounted for 64 per cent of the total dollar volume, and the top five companies accounted for 18 per cent.[10] The top company, Lockheed Aircraft Corporation, received awards of just over $1.5 billion, and three other companies received awards of over $1.0 billion each. The company in one hundredth place received awards totaling $40 million. The heavy concentration of awards to the leading companies has, however, been declining slowly but steadily in recent years.

Some changes in the list of one hundred top companies occur from year to year because of mergers and other corporate changes. One new joint venture in 1966, a merger of construction companies making military bases and installations, is in ninth place with contracts exceeding a half billion dollars.

Other changes reflect shifts in procurement patterns. The 1966 list contains companies in four new industrial categories—weapons, textiles and clothing, construction

9 Research Analysis Corporation, *Industrial Classification and Economic-Impact Analysis* (Study for Department of Defense, 1966), pp. 27–28.
10 "100 Companies and Their Subsidiary Corporations Listed According to Net Value of Military Prime Contract Awards, Fiscal Year 1966," Office of the Secretary of Defense, 1966.

equipment, and building supplies—and a substantial increase in the number of ammunition companies. These shifts obviously reflect the rising demands for conventional materiel for Vietnam.

Awards to small business concerns, generally defined as those with five hundred or fewer employees, comprise about one-fifth of the dollar volume of prime contracts. The percentage has fluctuated from a peak of 25 per cent in 1954 to a low of 16 per cent in 1963, rising since then to 21 per cent in 1966.[11]

Small business concerns are more likely to receive awards for textiles and clothing, weapons, construction, and miscellaneous equipment—the more conventional defense items. Not surprisingly, they receive very few prime contracts for work in aircraft or missiles. The current shift toward more conventional defense purchases for the Vietnam action improves the economic outlook for the small businesses, whereas likely future shifts toward strategic retaliatory weapons and intercontinental missile defenses would cause a decline in defense opportunities for small businesses.

Like industries, individual companies differ both according to their share of defense income and their reliance on defense income. A study by Murray Weidenbaum classified the top thirty-five companies in dollar volume of defense awards in 1962 according to the percentage those awards constituted of each firm's total sales.[12] Seven of these companies, all aircraft firms, re-

11 *Military Prime Contract Awards,* July–December, 1966, Office of the Secretary of Defense, pp. 11–13, 21.
12 Cited in Research Analysis Corporation, *Industrial Classification and Economic Impact Analysis, op. cit.,* p. 27.

ceived awards amounting to more than 75 per cent of
their total sales, whereas nine companies received awards
amounting to less than 25 per cent of their total sales.
Some companies received very substantial shares of the
total defense program but were nevertheless little dependent upon defense income in relation to civilian
sales. General Motors, for example, ranked tenth in
dollar volume of defense awards,[13] but these awards
constituted only 3 per cent of the company's total sales.
Near the other extreme was Lockheed, ranking first in
volume of awards and making 81 per cent of its total
sales to defense purchasers. The differences in degree
of military versus civilian diversification indicate the
complexities in attributing major roles to the defense
firms. One does not think of General Motors as a defense firm; yet it is a considerably heavier contributor
to the defense program in dollar volume than, for example, Grumman Aircraft, which most people do think
of as a defense firm.

The Regions Involved

For various reasons of climate, geography, economic
history, and accident, defense spending is unevenly distributed throughout the country. Shipbuilding takes
place in coastal locations, much aircraft and missile
work where climate permits all-year testing and launch-
ing. Large manufacturing firms are in dense population

13 Data on 1962 dollar volume of awards is from "100 Companies and Their Subsidiary Corporations Listed According
to Net Value of Military Prime Contract Awards, Fiscal Year
1962," Office of the Secretary of Defense, 1962.

areas, and large military installations are in outpost areas like Alaska and Hawaii.

The most common, but not the most accurate, measure of geographic distribution of defense spending is the Defense Department's annual report of military prime contract awards by region and state. The distribution for fiscal year 1966 ranges from 20.0 per cent for the Pacific Region down to only 0.4 per cent for Alaska and Hawaii. The Middle Atlantic Region is next highest, and the Mountain region next lowest. By states, California is far in the lead, followed by New York, Texas, Connecticut, and Pennsylvania.[14]

Data on dollar distribution of prime contracts alone do not give a clear picture of the actual impact of defense spending upon an area. The total size of the area's labor force, the number employed on contract awards, and the number in other defense-generated employment such as the servicing of large military bases all play an important role. A recent Department of Defense study attempted to measure the total impact by state more accurately by developing a "defense dependency ratio" —the ratio of total defense-generated employment to a state's total work force.[15] Results for mid-1966 showed that Alaska is the most dependent on defense spending, with 9.7 per cent of its work force engaged in defense-generated employment, mainly through military bases.

14 *Military Prime Contract Awards by Region and State,* Fiscal Years 1962–1966, Office of the Secretary of Defense, 1967, pp. 1–2.
15 Col. Vernon M. Buehler, USA, "Economic Impact of Defense Programs," *Defense Industry Bulletin* (March, 1967), pp. 1–12.

Alaska ranked forty-fourth among the states in prime contract awards in 1966. California, which ranked first in prime contract awards, is rated eighth in defense dependency, and New York, which ranked second in prime contract awards, drops all the way down to thirty-first place in defense dependency.

This study also surveyed the distribution of defense employment by state and region for major defense product groups. Results showed aircraft employment to be the most widely distributed among regions, with all except two getting at least 10 per cent of total aircraft employment. Missile and space employment, by contrast, is concentrated heavily in the three Pacific Coast states and the South Atlantic states. The Pacific states account for 26 per cent of all surveyed defense employment, and the region is unique in its substantial employment in every product group.

In a study published in 1966 by the Brookings Institution, Roger E. Bolton takes a somewhat different approach to the determination of defense impact by state and region.[16] He assumes that local income—income developed from within a state or region—is passive and that exogenous income—income from outside the state—is the primary determinant in the economic growth of an area. He classifies all defense purchases as exogenous income, and determines what percentage defense income represents of the total exogenous income of an area, and what the rate of growth of de-

16 Roger E. Bolton, *Defense Purchases and Regional Growth* (Washington: The Brookings Institution, 1966).

fense income has been in the area over a ten-year period. His findings indicate that the contribution of defense income to regional growth for the period 1952–1962 was greatest for the Mountain region, closely followed by the Pacific region. More modest growth impacts were found for five other regions, and two regions, Middle Atlantic and East North Central, suffered negative growth effects, primarily as a result of post-Korean war cutbacks. Unfortunately, as Bolton emphasizes, his conclusions are only estimates because of the unavailability of complete data, and the necessity for reliance solely upon prime contract figures. And, of course, his conclusions are already somewhat dated. But his model looks sufficiently promising that one might hope it will be brought up to date with the use of the more reliable data now becoming available.

Bolton also studies the concentration of various specific types of programs in certain geographical areas, and observes:

> Not only are some states heavily dependent on one or two programs, but in several cases this amounts to dependence on one or two companies. Examples are the Martin-Marietta Company in Colorado; United Aircraft and General Dynamics (Electric Boat Division) in Connecticut; Lockheed in Georgia; Boeing Company in Kansas and Washington; Bath Iron Works in Maine; Ingalls Shipbuilding Company in Mississippi; McDonnell Aircraft in Missouri; and Newport News Shipbuilding and Dry Dock Company in Virginia. In such cases, apprehension about the effects of dependence of certain

states and metropolitan areas on defense business is understandable, for these areas may suffer a great loss in demand even if the total defense budget is not cut.[17]

Effects of Subcontracting

Most of the foregoing data are based on first-order or prime contract distribution and do not reflect the impact of subcontracting. For some years various critics have expressed concern about the economic effects of the heavy concentration of prime contracts in relatively few industries and firms and in certain geographic areas. The standard reply has been that the prime contract figures exaggerate this apparent concentration and that figures on subcontracts, if only they were available, would show that subcontracting suffuses the impact broadly through other industries, smaller firms, different geographic areas.

Late in 1966 the Department of Defense completed its first detailed study of subcontracting procurement patterns.[18] Although the study had a number of limitations, it was certainly indicative of general trends. And it turned up some surprising results, results that overturned so many assumptions about subcontracting that one reliable business publication headed its account of the findings "End of a myth." [19] Some of the key findings were these:

17 *Ibid.*, p. 117.
18 C-E-I-R, INC., *Economic Impact Analysis of Subcontracting Procurement Patterns* (Study for Department of Defense, 1966).
19 *Business Week*, April 8, 1967.

• For all prime contractors, their top subcontractor accounts for an average of 36 per cent of all subcontract value and their top ten subcontractors account for an average of 80 per cent of all subcontract value.

• Many of the leading subcontractors are also important prime contractors. Eighteen of the twenty-six leading subcontractors are also among the top one hundred Department of Defense prime contractors.

• Subcontracting concentration by industry awaits further study, but a small sample study shows subcontracting concentration to be particularly heavy in missile and space programs, where the top ten subcontractors account for 92 per cent of the total subcontract value. By contrast, the top ten subcontractors in the aircraft and airframe program account for only 50 per cent of the total subcontract value.

• Perhaps most startling of all, geographic concentration appears to be even heavier for subcontract than for prime contract awards. The leading ten states in the prime contract series account for 67 per cent of total prime contract procurement, whereas the ten top states in the subcontract series receive over 75 per cent of all subcontract awards. Furthermore, eight of the top ten states appear on both lists. And California and New York, which rank first and second in both series, together account for over 40 per cent of the total value of subcontract awards.

These findings point up the need for much more sophisticated data and analysis in the field of economic impact of defense spending, and the pitfalls of operating on assumptions—however logical they might appear to be—rather than on hard facts.

OTHER DEFENSE EFFECTS
ON BUSINESS

Now I should like to comment briefly on several other ways in which the defense sector affects business.

Research and Development

As was noted earlier, a major characteristic of the present defense effort is its concentration on extending the frontiers of military technology. As a result, funds for so-called "research and development" have for the past fifteen years constituted a very substantial part of the total defense budget.

In contrast, with a few notable industrial exceptions, private industry in the United States spends very little on research and development of a fundamental sort. Civilian efforts are more likely to go into styling and minor product improvements rather than into basic advances in technology. This occurs, in part, because research costs are high and it is hard to protect property rights to successful innovations.

The large military expenditures for research and development help to make up in some measure and in some areas this deficit in civilian research spending. Military research and development, as Murray Weidenbaum points out, constitute one of the major growth areas of the American economy.[20] While military tech-

20 Murray L. Weidenbaum, "The Impact of Military Procurement on American Industry," in *Planning and Forecasting in the Defense Industries,* p. 150.

nology is the direct beneficiary of these expenditures, their results spread indirectly into many areas of non-defense output. Transport aircraft, cheap nuclear power, exploration of space, high speed computers and other electronic developments are just a few examples of the benefits of military research and development to the nation's general technological progress.

A precise measure of the impact of military research and development is impossible to determine, in part because definitions differ widely among the different sectors of the economy. In defense budgets, the research and development category includes not only basic and applied research, but the actual construction and testing of numbers of prototypes. Thus comparative data may give a misleading picture of the actual role of military research and development.

According to figures developed by the Bureau of the Budget and the National Science Foundation, two-thirds of all the research and development work in the entire nation is presently financed by the Department of Defense, NASA, and the AEC.[21] Defense-supported R and D was 57 per cent of the United States total in 1954 and had climbed to 65 per cent in the U.S. total by 1963. By 1965 the dollar amount had risen to almost $15 billion.

Most of this total goes directly for development of military hard goods. A breakdown of military prime contract awards for research and development in 1966 shows only 6 per cent allocated to basic research, a

21 *Report of the Committee on the Economic Impact of Defense and Disarmament, op. cit.,* Appendix Table 16, p. 87.

decline from 9 per cent in 1965 and 11 per cent in 1964.[22]

The largest military R and D contracts go, of course, to those industries which are closest to the frontiers of weapon development. By far the largest allocation presently goes to programs concerned with missile and space systems, followed by electronics and communications equipment and aircraft. R and D allocations as a percentage of total allocations have been falling for aircraft and electronics and communications programs in recent years, but climbing for missile and space programs.

Employment Patterns

The most notable defense impact upon employment patterns is the shift away from production workers and toward the technical, scientific, and managerial ranks. In 1960, production workers constituted 75 per cent of total employment in U.S. manufacturing. But the percentage of production workers to total employees in five major defense-oriented industries stood at 60 per cent. By 1964, production workers in these five industries had dropped to 57 per cent. Production workers by individual industry ranged from 84 per cent in ship and boat building and repairing to 41 per cent in ordnance and accessories (including missiles and space vehicles). A major manufacturer of aircraft and missiles

22 *Military Prime Contract Awards by Service Category and Federal Supply Classification,* Fiscal Years 1963–1966, Office of the Secretary of Defense, 1967, p. 2.

has estimated that his employment requirements for production workers will have dropped to 29 per cent by 1970.

This shift, of course, reflects the growth of research and development allocations and the resulting increase in technical and scientific employment in defense work, as well as the automation of many production processes. It has been estimated that the number of engineers and scientists employed in five major defense-oriented industries in 1962 constituted 31 per cent of the total of all scientists and engineers employed in all U.S. industries. The five industries employed 48 per cent of all physicists in U.S. industries.[23]

To help fill in gaps in the data on defense impact, the Department of Defense and NASA have jointly undertaken the collection of employment and other information from large defense contractors in a program called the Economic Information System (EIS). Data on defense-generated industrial employment trends from 1963 to 1966 for 150 EIS-surveyed plants were published in March, 1967.[24] They show that total defense-generated employment in these plants declined from 1963 to 1965 but began to rise again in 1966. Among product groups, the biggest decreases occurred in missiles (40 per cent) and electronics and communications (28 per cent). Significant percentage gains were shown by ships and by ammunition, although both of these product groups involved much smaller absolute numbers of employees.

23 *Report of the Committee on the Economic Impact of Defense and Disarmament, op. cit.,* Appendix Table 19, p. 89.
24 Col. Vernon M. Buehler, *op. cit.,* pp. 10–12.

The Oliver article cited earlier analyzes trends in defense-generated employment in several heavily defense-oriented industries from 1965 to 1967. The percentage of defense-generated employment dropped very slightly for aircraft and for communications equipment, and rose substantially for ordnance. Oliver points out that while defense purchases of aircraft and communications equipment rose during the period, civilian purchases in both fields rose even faster to produce the slight decline in percentages of defense employment.[25]

Changes in Procurement Policies

During the years immediately following the Korean War, at a time when major new weapons systems were being developed, there was increasing reliance by the Department of Defense on the cost-plus-fixed-fee contract. This type of contract rose from 20 per cent to a high of 38 per cent of all contract awards during the period 1956 to 1961. The argument for its use was that contractors venturing into relatively new weapons fields could not reasonably anticipate their costs and so should be reimbursed for actual costs incurred in the development and production of new military products.

The trouble with this type of contract, as Defense Secretary McNamara has pointed out, is that it "offers neither reward for good performance nor penalty for bad." [26] In 1961 the Defense Department undertook a

25 Richard P. Oliver, *op. cit.*, pp. 9–11.
26 Memorandum to the President from the Secretary of Defense, "Department of Defense Cost Reduction Program—Annual Progress Report," July 5, 1967, p. 7.

program to reduce use of this type of contract and to replace it with firm fixed price or incentive contracts and the widest possible price competition. The results have been notable. "Cost-plus" contracts declined from the high of 38 per cent in 1961 to 9.4 per cent in 1966 and have been held to 10.0 per cent thus far in 1967, even under the exigencies of procurement for the Vietnam war. Contracts awarded on the basis of competitive bidding have increased from 33 per cent to 47 per cent for the period from 1961 to 1967. Fixed price awards have increased from 44 per cent to 60 per cent, and incentive contracts have increased from 17 per cent to 28 per cent for the period.[27]

The actual economic effects of these changing procurement policies are difficult to measure. The Department of Defense claims that shifting the risk to the contractor and then compensating him fairly for that risk does indeed reward good performance and penalize bad, and saves the taxpayers many millions of dollars annually. Some industry representatives, on the other hand, claim that contractors are being forced to assume unwarranted risks, with the results that profits on defense contracts have dropped from 4.0 per cent in 1960 to 3.0 per cent in 1965 and 1966 and that the quality of military hardware is declining.

I might note that the risks contractors assume under the current procurement policies are generally the same they assume in any nondefense sector of the economy. The effect of "cost-plus" contracting tended to re-

27 Office of the Assistant Secretary of Defense, Installation and Logistics, August, 1967.

move rewards for initiative and ingenuity and to place many of management's normal decisions and prerogatives with service contracting officers, so that the contracting firms were halfway nationalized. The new policies return these contractors to the same economic basis of operations as that of any other kind of business activity in America.

A LOOK TO THE FUTURE

Predicting future trends is a risky undertaking at best, and I am no better qualified at soothsaying than the next man. I recall giving a speech in 1960 in which I remarked that a defense budget higher than $45 billion or lower than $40 billion in the near future was hard to imagine. Today, as we pass the $70 billion mark, I am comforted to recollect that I did add to that speech the qualification that greatly changed military budget levels were not only possible but likely since the defense sector was full of surprises.

It was, and it still is and will continue to be. Much depends, of course, on those totally unpredictable technological breakthroughs that can cause such major shifts in direction in so short a time. Even more depends on the state of the world around us—relations with Russia, developments in Red China, the state of affairs in Vietnam. Ruling out for the moment any momentous changes in these factors, are there any educated guesses we can make about the impact of the defense sector on American business over the next few years? I think there are a few worth attempting.

Strategic Retaliatory Forces

Expenditures for these forces declined in the early 1960's as major missile systems initiated earlier were brought to required levels of strength. My guess is that this trend will be reversed as we enter a new round of improvements. The recent news stories about new missiles with multiple warheads lend credence to this assumption. As I remarked earlier, the revolution in military technology is irreversible. So long as an external threat exists, we have no alternative but to attempt to maintain superiority over advances in military technology by the Communist nations. Improvements in our retaliatory weapons are now possible, and some are likely to be put into production.

Intercontinental Defense Forces

These are definitely slated for buildup, with Defense Secretary McNamara's announcement of the development of a thin anti-ballistic missile defense against possible attack from Red China. The real question is whether it will remain "thin" or whether it will have some tendency to become thicker with time. Other things remaining relatively equal, my guess is that some very gradual and limited thickening is likely to take place. Once a system is in operation, it is only natural to want to incorporate at least minor improvements, to build up some obvious weak spots. But a major expansion of the program should not occur unless other things do become unequal and Russia, for example, undertakes a heavy anti-missile defense program.

Conventional Weaponry

These levels would, of course, decline substantially if the Vietnam war comes to an end. But I would guess that we will continue a low-level program to keep these materiel modernized and to maintain a sound base for quick expansion of production should the need arise for their use in any other limited actions. The very ultimate nature of the destructive power of the new global weapons enforces limited military actions with conventional weapons as the only alternative to holocaust.

These several major trends would mean for business:

• Expanding shares of defense income for the aircraft and missile industries, both heavily involved in retaliatory and anti-missile defense programs. Future declines in manned aircraft would be offset by the aircraft industries' substantial involvement in missile production.

• Expanding shares of defense income for the electronics and communications industries. These manufacturers are involved not only in the so-called "flyaway" products—the planes and missiles—but they are heavily involved in the increasingly important "ground environment"—the warning systems, the landing and launch sites, the guidance control and communications centers.

• When Vietnam hostilities cease, a sharp decrease in shares of defense income for industries producing conventional weapons, but then a leveling-off to maintain an immediately available general purpose force.

Expanding shares of defense spending for research and development. These shares leveled off somewhat in recent years as major new weapon systems were brought from exploratory stages to actual production and operational readiness. A new round of technological advances will involve increases once more in R and D allocations.

A continuation of the shift in employment patterns from production to technical and scientific workers. The increasing automation of all of American industry will support this trend, and growing R and D allocations will continue to accentuate it in defense-oriented industries.

Continuing concentration of major contracts among a relatively small number of very large business firms. Global weapons and defense systems are necessarily limited in number and gigantic in size and complexity. If the government itself is not to assume major responsibility for weapons production, then major responsibility must be assigned to a relatively few firms for overall management of individual weapons systems. Some important subsections may be broken out for separate contracting. Much of the actual work will be subcontracted. But firms with annual contracts above the $1 billion level will continue as a highly significant part of the defense picture.

Continuing geographic concentration. Aircraft work is fairly evenly spread throughout the major regions of the country, but the other growth programs—missiles, electronics and communications, and research and development—are much more concentrated geographically. The Pacific region, ranking high already in most of these growth areas, may even increase its dominance. Relative gains will occur for the Middle and South Atlantic regions. The Mountain region may hold its own because of its missile work. Relative losses will be sharpest for the four Central regions (East and West, North and South).

The Problem of Cutbacks

The specter of drastic future cutbacks in the defense sector is one that I think is somewhat exaggerated, although it is certainly a subject for sober study. We managed to survive a huge cutback after World War II and a significant cutback after the Korean War, not without many instances of severe dislocation but certainly without dire harm to the economy as a whole. Hostilities in Vietnam do not appear likely to terminate with precipitate withdrawal of American forces. A more likely eventuality is a more or less gradual decrease in spending for Vietnam. These gradual cutbacks will affect primarily those industries which are not "defense industries"—that is, industries which have large non-defense markets—clothing, fuel and lubricants, vehicles, machinery. Most of them diverted production to defense needs as the Vietnam action expanded, and could probably redirect their output to civilian markets without major dislocations. One exception which may suffer serious cutback problems is the ammunition industry.

The heavily defense-oriented industries are those involved with the major global weapons and defense systems. Here the possibilities of cutbacks center on new disarmament agreements or on the shift to new weapon developments because of technological breakthroughs. Disarmament agreements are slow in coming and are likely to involve only one type of weapon system at a time. Shifts from one to another weapon system are likely to occur from time to time, but the same industries may be equipped to play at least some continuing roles in the newer systems. The obvious answer for defense-oriented industries is diversification—diversification both in the area of military products and in the direction of adapting their technological advances for civilian products. The defense industries are well aware of this. Lockheed, for example, currently has contracts for three military transport planes and a patrol bomber, is the principal prime contractor for the Polaris and Poseidon Missiles, and receives additional contracts for space vehicles, satellite control research, electronics, and shipbuilding—all this in addition to a substantial non-defense output.

Defense Department officials believe that the change in procurement policies from "cost-plus" to fixed price contracts following price competition has encouraged diversification—a firm which may lose a competition will be aggressive about developing other markets as a cushion. And a recent change in procurement regulations allows companies to charge to defense contracts certain costs associated with planning for diversification. While it does not permit research and development costs for new nondefense products, it does permit "costs of generalized long-range management planning which is concerned with the future overall development of the contractor's business and which may take into account the eventual possibility of economic dislocations or fundamental alterations in those markets in which the contractor currently does business." [28]

TWO POLICY QUESTIONS

I should like to conclude with a brief consideration of two important policy questions concerning the defense impact on American business.

Defense Procurement Policy

The general policy guiding defense purchases, simply stated, is to obtain the most for a given budget. No one argues with this as a general rule, but the question does arise as to whether there ought to be some exceptions, and on what grounds. Two other considerations are sometimes put forward to compete with the "least cost" policy. They are the "fair share" and the "social cost" considerations.

The "fair share" proponents are concerned about the heavy concentration of defense spending in some

28 Armed Services Procurement Regulation, revised, March 6, 1964.

geographic regions, some industries, and some firms—
usually not their own. A Senate bill cosponsored in
1959 by my distinguished predecessor in this lecture
series proposed a policy declaration by Congress that:

> . . . the security of the Nation requires that its
> economy, and the economy of each section of the
> country, be maintained at a level which can sup-
> port its programs for defense and sustain the private
> economic system . . .

> . . . in placing purchases under this chapter the
> procuring agency shall consider the strategic and
> economic desirability of allocating purchases to dif-
> ferent geographical areas of the Nation and to
> eligible suppliers from whom relatively small pro-
> portions of procurement have been purchased. . . .

Although Congress did not adopt this bill, it has
enacted one measure under the "fair share" criterion—
the special defense program to aid small business.

If the concentration of defense work increases, and
if the country's general economic health should dip, so
that alternative markets and employment sources are
not so readily available, the pressure for at least some
concessions to the "fair share" criterion is certain to
increase.

The "social cost" argument runs that some contracts
ought to be directed to economically distressed or labor
surplus areas as a means of keeping all parts of the
economy in sound health and as a means of saving other
and greater government costs in unemployment insurance, relief and welfare measures, and loss of taxes on
earned income. Congress has provided for some use of

the "social cost" criterion by a policy of special consideration to labor surplus areas—certain preferences are given to contractors who will have part of their work performed in these areas. To date, however, this program has had only very limited success. A major problem is that many labor surplus areas simply do not have the kind of capacity needed to produce defense items.

Certainly the defense budget is a large and powerful economic tool for the government, and one is tempted to seek its uses to solve an array of problems. But, other, more direct means are or can be made available to aid distressed areas. And sound economic principles would argue that those industries not getting their "fair share" of defense spending should develop markets where they can compete successfully rather than through artificial supports. Generally speaking, I think we are better off to stick close to the "least cost" policy in defense purchases. In the long run, the cost to the nation will be less if monies are used for direct rather than indirect purposes, and the public will be better informed of the actual costs of the programs among which it must allocate its support.

The "Military-industrial Complex"

In his farewell speech to the nation in 1961, President Eisenhower warned against "the acquisition of unwarranted influence, whether sought or unsought, by the military-industrial complex." Has there been such influence exercised by an alliance of military and industrial interests against the general interests of the broader public?

Certainly the large defense budget carries enormous potentials for such influence. A recent Associated Press survey of defense spending spoke of the "Pentagon's awesome power" and described the Department of Defense as "the mightiest concentration of economic power in the world today."

Suspicions of improper relationships between the military and some large defense firms are heightened by the frequency with which retired military officers once active in procurement areas or choices among weapons systems accept high positions with defense firms.

If I might speak half—but only half—facetiously, I sometimes think a truer picture is not of one giant military-industrial complex but of a whole array of little military-industrial complexes, each promoting its own service or branch of the service, its favored weapon, and its own firm, each cheerfully attempting to cut down all the competing little military-industrial complexes. The mutual backscratching that goes on among them is more likely to be outdone by the backstabbing. I think it likely that the safety of the general interest lies in large part in the fierce competition among the many special interests that comprise the supposedly monolithic military-industrial complex.

One way or another, we must produce the defense products essential to our survival in today's world. The only alternative to our present system would be the nationalization of weapons production. Then we might be faced with the "military complex, period" or perhaps with the "military-bureaucratic complex." I for one would not choose either of those alternatives.

But there are some things we can do to lessen the possible threats to the public interest from the military-industrial complex or complexes. We can continue and extend the current shift toward price competition in defense contracting. We might adopt a policy to discourage former military or Defense Department personnel from accepting positions with firms over which they had exercised some power of decision in weapon selection or other procurement activities. We should insist on continuing our strong Constitutionally-based civilian control over military affairs, with the maximum number of budgetary decisions based on the disinterested results of systems analysis rather than on the special pleadings of any alliance of military and industrial groups.

The defense sector today is large and continuing. Its impact on American business is substantial. Properly regulated, it will continue to provide for the nation's military might without undermining either our economic strength or our democratic institutions in the years to come.

THE DEFENSE SECTOR:
AN EVALUATION OF ITS
ECONOMIC AND SOCIAL IMPACT

by Arthur F. Burns

IN HIS FAMOUS farewell address, President Eisenhower warned the nation to remain vigilant of what he called "the military-industrial complex." This warning needs to be remembered and pondered by thoughtful citizens. An age of nuclear weapons leaves no time for assembling the military and industrial forces needed to repel an aggressor. Once a nation is attacked, it can be practically destroyed in a matter of minutes. For this reason as well as because of the unhappy state of our relations with the Communist bloc, "normalcy" for us has come to include since 1950 a formidable military establishment in a state of constant readiness, if need be, for war. But "the conjunction of an immense military establishment and a large arms industry," as President Eisenhower has observed, "is new in the American experience. The total influence—economic, political, even spiritual—is felt in every city, every statehouse, every office of the Federal government." My purpose today is to consider with you some of the ways in which the emergence of a massive and permanent defense sector has already changed and is continuing to change our economic and social life.

I

To begin with, the defense sector has revolutionized governmental finances in our generation. In fiscal year 1948, Federal expenditures came to $36 billion. In fiscal 1964, well before Vietnam became a significant financial burden, spending on national defense alone amounted to $54 billion, or half as much again as the total budget in 1948. In the current fiscal year, the defense budget may amount to about $80 billion, but this huge sum still does not indicate the full financial cost of defense activities. The Federal government expects to spend another $5 billion on international programs and also $5.25 billion on space research and technology. These activities, of course, are mainly pursued in the interests of our national security. Moreover, the Federal budget allows $10.5 billion for interest on the public debt and over $6.5 billion for veterans' benefits, the former being preponderantly and the latter entirely a legacy of past wars. Thus, defense-related expenditures will probably come this year to over $100 billion—a sum that represents more than $500 for every man, woman, and child of our population.

The large and rising cost of defense activities would have caused financial problems even if other costs of government had not changed. In fact, as we all know, the range of governmental activities has greatly increased. Since the end of World War II, the American people have come to expect their government to maintain economic conditions that are generally conducive to full employment. The Federal government has been also under increasing pressure to enlarge social services —that is to say, improve the nation's schools, help support universities, improve hospitals and medical facilities, facilitate home ownership, reduce urban slums, promote safer and faster air travel, raise social security and related welfare benefits, train manpower for the needs of industry, seek ways of reducing air and water pollution, and even concern itself with problems of traffic congestion and police protection. These expanding interests of the Federal government are a political response to the increasing urbanization of modern life, the new opportunities opened up by advances in technology, and the growing impatience for better living on the part of many citizens who have been left behind by the march of progress. Thus, at the very stage of history when demographic, technological, and political trends have been releasing powerful forces to raise the costs of government, the defense sector likewise became an increasing burden on the Treasury. The inevitable result has been a vast growth of Federal spending— from $36 billion in fiscal 1948 to $120 billion in 1964, and probably $175 billion, if not more, this fiscal year.

The upsurge of Federal spending on defense and on civilian activities has naturally resulted in much higher taxes. To be sure, we have recently become ac-

customed to deficits when the economy is booming as
well as when the economy is depressed. The role of
deficits in governmental finance, however, is commonly
exaggerated. From mid-1946 to June, 1967, the cumula-
tive revenue of the Federal government covered all but
2 per cent of its expenditures, so that Federal taxes
have in fact grown just about as rapidly as expenditures. Our economy has also grown substantially during
this period, but not enough to prevent taxes from siphon-
ing off an increasing portion of the national income. In
fiscal 1940, Federal revenues came to about 7 per cent
of the gross national product, in 1950 to 15.5 per cent,
in 1960 to 19 per cent, last year to 20 per cent. Meanwhile, state and local taxes have also moved up—indeed,
they have grown even more rapidly during the past ten
or twenty years than Federal taxes. According to the
national income accounts, the combined revenue of all
governmental units amounted in the past fiscal year to
about 29 per cent of the gross national product and 32
per cent of the net national product; and even the higher
figure may understate the tax burden, since it makes
inadequate allowance for the capital used up in the
process of producing goods and services.

This year, with the war in Vietnam escalating and
social expenditures also rising, the Federal budget deficit
may well exceed $20 billion unless steps are taken to
raise taxes and curb expenditures. To reduce the enormous deficit now in sight, President Johnson has proposed a 10 per cent surcharge on income taxes, but
the Congress has thus far failed to adopt the proposal.
Some members of Congress feel that the tax burden is

already so heavy that it would be wiser to cut governmental expenditures than to raise taxes. Others would be willing to accept higher taxes provided substantial reductions in expenditures were simultaneously made. With financial markets disturbed and interest rates rising above last year's abnormally high level, a great debate is now raging both within and outside governmental circles about the relation of the Federal budget to economic activity, interest rates, and inflation. What is critically at issue in this debate is not whether Federal spending should be permitted to rise, but the size of the reduction—if any—in the projected scale of spending on nondefense programs. No matter how this issue is resolved, spending in the aggregate will still go up, and —if history is any guide—taxes will follow; so that we now face the prospect of higher income taxes besides higher social security taxes and assorted increases of state and local taxes.

We also face the prospect of paying more for foodstuffs, clothing, automobiles, and whatever else we buy. The causes of inflation are complex, and it is never strictly true that an increase in spending on defense or on business equipment or on any other category is the sole cause of inflation. In principle, the government can always adjust its monetary and fiscal policies to economic conditions so as to keep the price level reasonably stable. If the government had foreseen how rapidly the cost of the Vietnam war would mount and if it had taken promptly the restraining measures needed to keep the aggregate demand for goods and services from outrunning the nation's capacity to produce, the new round of inflation that we have experienced since 1964 could have been prevented. But if we blame the government for its lack of foresight or courage in this instance, we should also bear in mind that the theoretical ideal of price stability has rarely, if ever, been closely approximated under wartime conditions.

When demand presses hard on a nation's resources, as it generally does at a time of war, it becomes very difficult to adjust tax, credit, and expenditure policies on the scale needed to prevent advances in the price level. The doubling of wholesale prices between 1940 and 1950 was obviously linked to the enormous expansion of military spending during World War II. Since then, the trend of prices has continued upward at a much slower pace, and no single factor stands out so prominently among the causes of inflation. Indeed, prices have risen less in our country since 1950 than in most others, despite our exceptionally large military burden. It is nevertheless true that the greater part of the recent advance in both wholesale and consumer prices came in three spurts—between 1950 and 1952 when the Korean War was raging, between 1955 and 1957 when a fairly rapid increase of military contracts for newly developed weapon systems paralleled a booming trend of business investment in new plant and equipment, and since mid-1965 when our ground forces shifted to an active role in Vietnam. It appears, therefore, that the sudden surges within the defense sector have contributed to the inflationary trend which has been gradually eroding all savings accumulated in the form of bank deposits, life insurance, savings bonds, and other fixed-income assets, besides complicating life for everyone whose money income fails to respond to the rising cost of living.

The defense sector has also contributed to the deficit in our balance of payments. Since 1950 the receipts from our sale of goods, services, and securities to foreign countries have run considerably below the sums that we need to pay foreign countries. One reason for this persistent deficit is the large expenditure that is required, year in and year out, to maintain our military forces abroad. Foreign assistance programs have also been adding to the deficit, although their foreign exchange cost is now much smaller. Since the revenue derived from our foreign transactions has been insufficient to cover the required payments, our stocks of gold have shrunk from $24.5 billion at the beginning of 1950 to about $13 billion at present. Meanwhile, the dollar balances that are held here by foreigners have also grown, so that the United States finds itself in the position of a banker whose short-term liabilities are steadily rising while his reserves keep dwindling. In order to check the deterioration in our international financial position, the Department of Defense has lately been favoring domestic over foreign suppliers even at cost differentials of 50 per cent. More disturbing still, the government has found it necessary to impose restrictions on the outflow of capital—an interference with private investment that is contrary to our national traditions. Even so, the deficit in the balance of payments has persisted, and—at least partly as a result of the war in Vietnam—it is larger this year than last. International confidence in the dollar, which is of such immense importance to America's political leadership as well as to our economy and that of the rest of the world, is still strong, but we can no longer count on it as we did ten or twenty years ago.

II

I have been concerned thus far with the financial aspects of national defense—its impact on governmental expenditures, taxes, the price level, and the balance of payments. Financial transactions and the price system, however, are merely mechanisms for putting a nation's resources to work and for distributing what is produced among people and their government. The resources that we devote to national defense are not available for making consumer goods or for adding to the stock of industrial equipment or for public uses in the sphere of education, health, or urban redevelopment. To the extent that we allocate labor, materials, and capital to national defense, we cannot satisfy our desires for other things. The civilian goods and services that are currently foregone on account of expenditures on national defense are, therefore, the current real cost of the defense establishment.

This cost has become very large, as my observations on governmental finance have already suggested. Its magnitude can perhaps be grasped best by considering the amount of labor devoted to national defense. In fiscal 1965, the armed forces numbered close to 2.75 million. They were supported by over 900,000 civilian workers attached to the Department of Defense and by another

2.1 million civilians employed in private industry who worked, directly or indirectly, on military supplies. Thus the total employment on defense goods and services amounted to 5.75 million, or to 86 out of every 1,000 employed workers in the country. Two years later—that is, during the fiscal year which ended June, 1967—the number was nearly 7.5 million, or 103 out of every 1,000 employed workers. The employment currently attributable to national security expenditures is still larger; for the figures that I have cited, besides not being fully up to date, take no account of the activities of the Atomic Energy Commission, the National Aeronautics and Space Administration, or other defense-related efforts.

A mere count of numbers, moreover, does not convey adequately the drain of the defense establishment on the nation's work force. Men differ in quality, and we need to take account of the fact that those involved in the defense effort are, on the average, superior from an economic viewpoint to workers engaged in civilian production. Military technology and operations have become very sophisticated in our times. The armed forces now have a highly skilled core and are very selective in accepting men for service. Indeed, the proportion of personnel who completed high school is much larger in the armed forces than in the comparable age group of the civilian population, while the proportion of college graduates is not materially lower. Training and skill count even more heavily among the civilians involved in defense activities. Last year, professional workers accounted for nearly 16 per cent and skilled blue-collar workers for 21 per cent of the civilians employed on defense work, in contrast to about 13 per cent for each of these groups in the total working population. One out of every five of the nation's electrical and mechanical engineers in civilian jobs, two out of every five airplane mechanics, two out of every five physicists outside of teaching, and three out of every five aeronautical engineers were employed on defense goods during the past year. And even these figures understate the skill dimension of defense employment, for they again leave out of account the highly technical activities originating in the Atomic Energy Commission and the Space Administration.

The heavy emphasis on skill and brainpower in defense employment reflects, of course, the explosion of military technology to which modern science has been contributing so much of its finest energy. Since the Korean War, defense contractors have been devoting themselves not only to the production of extremely complex weapons but also to developing entirely new weapon systems that no one as yet knew how to produce. Much of the defense sector of our economy has come to consist, therefore, of research and development work. The President's budget for this fiscal year, for example, allots about $16 billion to research and development, of which $9 billion is to be devoted to defense and another $5 billion to space activities. Since 1960 defense and space programs have consistently accounted for over 80 per cent of the rapidly increasing Federal funds devoted to research and development. More important still, they have amounted to about 54 per cent of the expenditure on research and development carried out in the entire nation—that is, by the Federal government, industry, universities and colleges, research centers affiliated with universities, and other nonprofit institutions. During the 1950's the proportion of the nation's research and development effort devoted to defense-related activities was only a little lower.

By diverting to its interest so much manpower, especially scientific and engineering skills, the defense establishment has left its mark on both the structure and the functioning of our economy. The effects are all around us. Some defense-oriented industries—notably, the aerospace group, electronics, and communications—have become a major factor in the economy, and their development has favored many communities—for example, Los Angeles, San Diego, Seattle, Baltimore. Some large firms have acquired marvelous technological competence from their work on defense or space contracts and this rather than any immediate profit has commonly been their chief reason for wanting the contracts in the first place. Not a few of the scientists and engineers who received their training in the more sophisticated enterprises have moved into traditional lines of activity, bringing something of the spirit of research and innovation with them. Many of the men released by the armed forces have been able to put the technical skills acquired during their military service to effective use in civilian jobs. Nondefense activities have shared in the increased supply of engineers, scientists, and technicians that has been stimulated by the defense-related demand. And not a few of the processes or products developed for the military have found application in civilian life—for example, jet transports, advanced computers, radar, miniaturized components, and nuclear power plants.

But if the defense sector has stimulated economic development in some directions, it has retarded growth in others. Many civilian-oriented laboratories of business firms have found it difficult to match the salaries or the equipment that subsidized defense firms offer to scientists and engineers. Research and development work in behalf of new products and processes for the civilian economy has therefore been handicapped. Small firms have derived little benefit from military or space contracts. The draft has added to the labor turnover of all businesses, large and small. The lack of opportunity in the defense sector for poorly educated and unskilled workers has not helped the rural Negroes who have flocked into the cities in recent years in search for jobs and a better life. Moreover, a new class of business executives has arisen, consisting of men whose understanding of marketing and cost controls is often deficient, but who know how to negotiate effectively with government officials handling military or scientific problems. While knowing the right people or having friends in the right places can sometimes advance the interests of an enterprise better than plain business ability, the nation's economic efficiency is not likely to reap a corresponding advantage.

In any event, the economic growth of a nation is a blind concept unless we consider what is produced as well as the rate of growth of what happens to be produced. During the decade from 1957 to 1966, our nation spent approximately $520 billion on defense and space programs. This sum is almost two-and-one-half times as large as the entire amount spent on elementary and secondary education, both public and private. It is two-and-three-quarter times as large as the amount spent on the construction of new housing units. It exceeds by over a fourth the expenditure on new plant and equipment by the entire business community—manufacturing firms, mining concerns, transportation enterprises, public utilities, and all other businesses. To be sure, an extra billion dollars' worth of bombs or missiles will increase current production just as much as an extra billion of new equipment for making civilian goods. Bombs or missiles, however, add nothing to the nation's capacity to produce, while new equipment serves to augment production in the future. The real cost of the defense sector consists, therefore, not only of the civilian goods and services that are currently foregone on its account; it includes also an element of growth that could have been achieved through larger investment in human or business capital. But even if we assumed that the conflicting influences of the defense sector on economic growth canceled out, its real cost is still enormous.

Unhappily, we live in dangerous times which make large national security expenditures practically unavoidable. Nevertheless, there are always some options in a nation's foreign and military policy, and we therefore must be alert to the opportunities that our military establishment forces us to forego. For example, if the resources devoted to military and space activities during the past decade had been put instead to civilian uses, we could surely have eliminated urban slums, besides adding liberally to private investment in new plant and equipment as well as to both public and private investment in human capital.

III

It follows from our analysis that the military-industrial complex, of which President Eisenhower spoke so perceptively in his farewell address, has not only been enlarging the scale of governmental operations and thereby complicating financial problems. By changing the thrust of economic activity and by making the economy more dependent on government, it has also been affecting profoundly the character of our society. Nor have the social effects been confined to the kinds of goods that we produce. Hopefulness about the future, optimism about success of new undertakings, impatience to complete satisfactorily whatever is begun—these psychological qualities have been peculiarly American characteristics, and they account in far greater degree than we may realize for the remarkable achievements of our economic system and the vigor of our political democracy. These qualities are deep-rooted in American experience and they continue to sustain us. Nevertheless, the development and spread of thermonuclear weapons, the frustrations of the cold war, and now the brutal struggle in Vietnam have left us, despite our awesome military power, more anxious about our national security than our fathers or grandfathers ever were.

Adults whose habits were formed in an earlier generation may put the dangers of nuclear catastrophe out of mind by losing themselves in their work or by seeking solace in religion. That is more difficult for our children who increasingly wonder what kind of world they have inherited by our doings. There can be little doubt that the lively competition among the great powers in devising instruments of terror is one of the underlying causes of the restlessness of modern youth.

Moreover, young men of military age are bearing a disproportionately large part of the defense burden. That is unavoidable at a time of war, but our generation has institutionalized compulsory military service even when the nation is at peace. It is undoubtedly true that many young men derive deep satisfaction from helping to protect their country by serving as soldiers, sailors, or aviators. Not only that, many have also found useful careers in the armed forces, or have benefited in their civilian jobs from the skills and discipline acquired during military service, or have gained a larger understanding of life by associating with men of widely different backgrounds or by being stationed abroad for a time. But just as these benefits deserve recognition, so too does the fact that the draft has by and large proved to be a seriously upsetting factor in the lives of young people. Not knowing when they would be called up for military service or whether they would be accepted, many have found themselves marking time. Those who are accepted have often had to interrupt their schooling or careers, perhaps alter plans with regard to marriage, and in any event be content with substantially lower pay than they could earn as a rule in civilian work. Moreover, the administration of the draft over the years, particularly the handling of student deferments, has raised troublesome moral questions in the minds of young people—and, for that matter, in the minds of older citizens as well.

The emergence of our country as a great military power, having world-wide political responsibilities, has also affected our educational system. Greater emphasis on science, mathematics, and modern languages in secondary schools and colleges, new area institutes and schools of international affairs in the universities, advanced courses in the esoteric languages and customs of the Far East and Africa—these educational developments not only reflect the widening scientific and geographic interests of modern business; they are also a response to urgent requirements of national security. But it is in the area of research, rather than teaching, where the impact of the defense establishment on our universities has been particularly felt. Colleges, universities, and research centers associated with universities spent in the aggregate $460 million on the performance of research and development in 1953, with something over half of this sum financed by the Federal government. Last year, the sum so spent was six-and-one-half times as large, and the federally-financed portion rose to 70 per cent. Clearly, Federal funds are mainly responsible for the extraordinary growth of research activities in universities, and the chief—although by no means the sole—reason for this governmental involvement is the intensive search for new knowledge on the part of defense-related agencies. During 1963–1966, the Department of Defense, the Atomic Energy Commission, and the Space Administration together accounted for five-eighths of the dollar value of Federal grants for research and development to institutions of higher learning, and their proportion in immediately preceding years was even larger.

The huge influx of governmental research funds has served to enrich the intellectual life of numerous colleges and universities, especially in the larger institutions where the grants have been mainly concentrated. By virtue of research grants, professors have better equipment to work with and more technical assistance than they had in former times. They also travel more, keep in closer contact with their counterparts in other universities, and mingle more freely with government officials, business executives, and scientists working for private industry. The gulf that previously separated a university from the larger interests of the community and the nation has therefore narrowed very significantly.

However, governmental research grants have created problems for universities as well as new opportunities for useful service. The greater interest of a faculty in research is not infrequently accompanied by lesser devotion to teaching. No little part of the time set aside for research may in practice be consumed by travel and conferences of slight scientific value. However welcome grants from military and space agencies may be, their concentration on the physical and engineering sciences makes it more difficult for a university to maintain the balance among various branches of learning that is so essential to the intellectual and moral improvement of man. Some military contracts involve classified research, and the secrecy which attends such work introduces an entirely foreign note in institutions that have traditionally taken a strong pride in completely free and uninhibited communication among scholars. Not less serious is the tendency, which appears to be growing among university scholars, to forsake the research to which they are drawn by intellectual curiosity in favor of projects that have been designed by, or contrived to suit the tastes of, government officials or others who take care of the financing. All universities and many of our colleges are struggling with this and other problems that the defense sector has created or accentuated.

The danger of diminished independence is not confined to research activities. If college or university presidents no longer speak out as vigorously on national issues as they did a generation or two ago, one major reason is that the institutions over whose destiny they preside have become heavily dependent on Federal contracts and subsidies. Even professors who are benefiting from Federal research grants or consulting relationships, or who expect to be able to do so in the future, have been learning the occasional value of studied reticence. And if discretion is tempering the spirit of forthright questioning and criticism in our universities, its power is all the stronger in the business world. It is hardly in the interest of businessmen to criticize their customers publicly, and by far the largest customer of the business world is clearly the Federal government itself.

Some firms sell all and many sell a good part of what they produce to the Federal government, and there are always others that hope to be in a position to do likewise in the future.

To be sure, the great majority of business executives, even those who manage very large enterprises, prefer commercial markets to governmental business; but they have become so sensitive nowadays to the regulatory powers of government that they rarely articulate their thoughts on national issues in public. Trade union leaders are typically more candid and outspoken on governmental issues than business executives; but they too have become dependent in varying degrees on the goodwill of government officials and therefore often deem tact or reticence the better part of wisdom. Not only that, but it is no longer unusual for the government in power, whether the administration be in Democratic or Republican hands, to suggest to prominent businessmen, trade union leaders, attorneys, journalists, or university professors that they support publicly this or that administration proposal. And men of public distinction at times comply regardless of their beliefs, perhaps because they are flattered by the attention accorded them, or because they vaguely expect some advantage from going along, or simply because they feel that they dare not do otherwise. Thus the gigantic size to which the Federal government has grown, for which the defense sector bears a heavy but by no means exclusive responsibility, has been tending to erode perceptibly, although not yet alarmingly as the open discussion of the war in Vietnam indicates, the spirit of rational and constructive dissent without which a democracy cannot flourish.

The huge size of military budgets and incomplete disclosure concerning their management carry with them also the danger of political abuse. Since money spent in the interest of national security necessarily has economic effects, the government in power may sometimes be tempted to ease domestic problems by adjusting the scale or direction of military spending. For example, raw materials may be stockpiled beyond the minimum military target, or the target itself may be revised upward, in order to grant some relief to a depressed industry. Or at a time of general economic slack, the government may begin to look upon military spending as if it were a public works program. Worse still, considerations of political advantage may play a role in deciding whether contracts are placed in one area rather than another, or with this firm instead of that. Such practices confuse military officers, lead to waste, and might even exacerbate international relations. Nevertheless, they are not entirely unknown to history, including our own. Fortunately, our government officials have generally been reluctant to tamper with something so fundamental to the nation as its defense establishment; and even on the rare occasions when they have strayed from virtue, the sluggishness of a governmental bureaucracy in carrying out any plan has kept down the scale of mischief. But if politics is ever effectively computerized, as some students believe it will be, we may have less protection against political abuse within the defense sector in the future.

Any enlargement of the economic power of government, whether brought about by military expenditures or through other causes, can eventually result in some infringement of liberty. However, because of the sense of urgency in troubled times, the requirements of national security may lead more directly to restriction of freedom. Necessary though the draft may be, it still constitutes compulsion of the individual by the state. Necessary though security clearances may be, they still constitute an invasion of privacy. Necessary though passport regulations may be, they still restrict the freedom of individuals to travel where they choose. Fortunately, the vitality of our democracy has thus far proved sufficient to limit restrictions of freedoms such as these. Not only that, it has enabled us to put an end to the nightmare of McCarthyism, to suppress the interest of the Central Intelligence Agency in our colleges and universities, and even to fight the war in Vietnam without imposing price and wage controls. We cannot take it for granted, however, that our formidable defense establishment will not give rise to more serious dangers to our liberties and the democratic process in the future.

IV

Throughout the ages, philosophers and religious teachers have lamented the horrors of war and searched for the keys to peace. Yet their noblest thought has been frustrated by the course of human events. Our country has been more fortunate than most, but we have had our share of the destruction of life and property that is the universal coin of warfare. Every American of age fifty or over has lived through two world wars, the Korean War, and now the smaller but still very costly and protracted struggle in Vietnam. When this war ends, military expenditures will probably decline for a while, as they have in fact after every war in our history. We cannot look forward, however, to demobilization on anything like the scale experienced after World War I or World War II, when the military budget was reduced by about 90 per cent within three years.

The reason for the difference, of course, is that the cold war is still with us, just as it was when the Korean hostilities ended. After the cessation of that conflict, the defense budget was reduced merely by a fifth. If the cost of the Vietnam War remains at approximately the current rate, it is doubtful whether a ceasefire will be followed by a reduction of even the Korean magnitude. A return to the defense budget of fiscal 1964 or 1965 would indeed involve a cut of roughly 35 per cent from this year's expenditure; but in the absence of a dramatic change in our international relations, this is quite unlikely. In the first place, prices are higher at present than they were in 1964 or 1965, and they will probably be higher still when the war phases out. In the second place, it may well be necessary for us to keep many more troops in Vietnam after a ceasefire than was the case in Korea and also to become more heavily involved in the task of reconstruction. In the third place, while stocks of military equipment were built up during the Korean War, they have been seriously depleted—particularly for the Reserve and National Guard units—by Vietnam. They will need to be rebuilt when hostilities come to an end, and this demand will be reinforced by the deferred procurement of newer models to replace equipment now in inventory.

Nevertheless, a sizeable reduction of military spending will take place in the year or two after the cease-fire, and we will have the opportunity to concentrate more of our resources on the arts of peace. In the past, the American economy has demonstrated a remarkable ability to adjust speedily to cutbacks in military spending, and we can be confident of doing so again. After World War I the conversion from war to peace was carried out with only a mild and brief setback in total economic activity. The like happened after World War II, despite the fact that more than two-fifths of our nation's resources were devoted to military uses at the peak of the war. Between 1945 and 1946, spending on the manufacture of defense goods dropped drastically and the number of men in the armed forces declined from 11.5 million to 3.5 million. Nevertheless, the unemployment rate remained below 4 per cent. The termination of the Korean War was followed by a recession but the return of peace was not its sole cause. In any event, unemployment during this recession was less serious at its worst than during the recession which came just before or just after it. With the experience that our country has gained during the past two decades in coping with economic fluctuations, with both the Executive and the Congress obviously eager to prevent unemployment, and with plans for dealing with post-Vietnam problems already beginning to take shape, there should not be much difficulty in adjusting Federal tax, expenditure, and credit policies so as to maintain aggregate monetary demand at the level needed to assure reasonably full employment when hostilities cease. Some sizeable adjustments will still need to be made by numerous communities and industries; but even they should prove manageable since the military cutbacks are likely to be largely concentrated on items produced by business firms that are closely oriented to our diversified and resilient civilian markets.

The highly specialized aerospace, electronics, and communications industries will probably not bear much of the burden of post-Vietnam cutbacks. Indeed, once the curve of military spending turns upward again, as it well may two or three years after the ceasefire, these are the very industries that are likely to benefit most from the dynamism of modern technology. To maintain a sufficient strategic superiority to deter any aggressor, we have been devoting vast sums to research and development, as I have already noted. The fantastic new weapons and weapon systems devised by our scientists and engineers soon render obsolete some of the existing devices, which themselves were new and revolutionary only a short time ago. But until the new devices are ready, those that were only recently new cannot be abandoned and may even need to be augmented. Meanwhile, strategic concepts may shift, as they did during

the sixties from reliance on massive nuclear deterrents
to developing a capability for limited warfare and coun-
terinsurgency operations. One way or another, therefore,
costs tend to multiply all around. The Soviet Union, of
course, will not stand still while our military prowess
increases. On the contrary, it is striving through a re-
markably enterprising and inventive military-industrial
complex of its own to establish military parity, if not
actual supremacy. For example, we have recently learned
of the deployment of an anti-ballistic missile system
around Moscow and Leningrad, of a novel ship-to-ship
missile of Russian origin fired in the Mediterranean, and
of the apparent development of an orbital bomb capability by the Soviet Union. Communist China has also
been developing, and with greater speed than was generally anticipated, the ability to make and deliver sophisticated weapons. In turn, our military establishment,
besides innovating vigorously on its own, keeps devising
countermeasures to what the Russians or Chinese have
or may have in hand. Both its reaction and its fresh
challenge to potential aggressors can be expected to become stronger once Vietnam no longer requires top
priority.

As we look beyond the cessation of hostilities in
Vietnam, we therefore need to recognize that the scale
of defense expenditures has, to a significant degree, become a self-reinforcing process. Its momentum derives
not only from the energy of military planners, contractors, scientists, and engineers. To some degree it is
abetted also by the practical interests and anxieties of
ordinary citizens. Any announcement that a particular

defense installation will be shut down, or that a particular defense contract will be phased out, naturally causes concern among men and women who, however much they abhor war and its trappings, have become dependent for their livelihood on the activity whose continuance is threatened. With a large part of our economy devoted to defense activities, the military-industrial complex has thus acquired a constituency including factory workers, clerks, secretaries, even grocers and barbers. Local politicians and community leaders may not find it easy to plead for the extension of activities that no longer serve a military purpose. Many, nevertheless, manage to overcome such scruples. Indeed, candidates for the Congress have been known to claim that they are uniquely qualified to ward off military closings or even to bring new contracts to their districts, and their oratory has not gone unrewarded by the electorate. The vested interest that numerous communities have acquired in defense activities may therefore continue to run up costs on top of the rising budgets generated by the momentum of competing military technologies.

If this analysis is at all realistic, the military-industrial complex will remain a formidable factor in our economic and social life in the calculable future. It will continue to command a large, possibly even an increasing, part of our resources. It will continue to strain Federal finances. It will continue to test the vigor of our economy and the vitality of our democratic institutions. It will continue to confuse understanding by suggesting to many foreign citizens, as it sometimes does even to our own, that our national prosperity is based on huge

military spending, when in fact we could be much more
prosperous without it. For all these reasons, while we
need to recognize the high and honorable national purpose of our military-industrial complex, we also need to
remain continually vigilant of its activities and seek to
protect ourselves against its possible abuses, just as we
long ago learned to guard the public interest against
business monopolies and as we are beginning to protect
ourselves against labor monopolies.

V

The scale and activities of our defense sector are
now being subjected to a searching public discussion.
Two major schools of political thought have become
locked in a contest for the mind and soul of America.
One school draws much of its strength from the revolution of military technology, the other from the revolution of rising expectations. One school tends to regard
communism as a centrally directed conspiracy that
threatens our survival as a free people. The other school
believes that communism is breaking up into indepen-
dent national movements, and sees the main threat to
free institutions in the deterioration of our cities and
the sickness of our society. One school seeks overwhelm-
ing military power to deter fresh Communist adven-
tures, and is willing to risk war in order to prevent the
geographic expansion of communism. The other school
seeks wider social justice and better economic conditions
for Negroes and others who have not participated fully
in the advance of prosperity, and holds that the force

of moral example can contribute more to our national security than additional bombs or missiles.

Both schools have focused attention on the Federal budget and neither has been satisfied by the treatment accorded its claims. From 1955 to 1965, Federal spending on nondefense activities increased faster than spending on defense. Since then, defense expenditures have gone up more rapidly, though not much more rapidly. Looking to the future, professional economists never tire of pointing out that our growing economy will make it possible to have more butter and, if they are needed, also more guns, even as we have been managing to do while the war in Vietnam is being waged. Their reassurance, however, does not satisfy those who feel that our national security requires not just more guns, but many more guns, and that we therefore need to give up some of our butter. Nor does it satisfy those who feel that we need not just more butter, but much more butter, and that our statistics of the gross national product are misleading us by their failure to allow for the pollution of our water, the poisons in our air, the noise of our streets, the rats in our slums, the rioting in our cities, and the destruction of life on our highways. Debate along these lines has reached a high pitch of intensity and even bitterness as the war in Vietnam has dragged out. It has become a divisive force, and it has brought anguish to our people. Its effect on the conduct of the war, however, is likely to count for less than its effect on the general direction of our foreign and military policy in the future.

For the debate is demonstrating to thoughtful citizens that our national security depends not only on awesome military forces. It depends also on the strength of our economic system, on the wholesomeness of our social and political life, and particularly on how well governmental objectives express the national will and purpose. As this lesson sinks in, we will want to try far harder than we ever have, both in our personal capacity and through our government, to bring the armaments race under decent control. And if the cracks of freedom within the Communist system of tyranny widen, as they well may in coming decades, we can count on being joined in this quest by the people of the Soviet Union and eventually by the people of mainland China as well. That, at any rate, is the only real basis for hope of saving ourselves and the entire human family from catastrophe.

Appendix

LIBERTY IS AT STAKE

FAREWELL ADDRESS

by Dwight D. Eisenhower

PRESIDENT OF THE UNITED STATES
DELIVERED TO THE NATION, WASHINGTON, D.C.,
January 17, 1961

GOOD EVENING, MY FELLOW AMERICANS: First, I should like to express my gratitude to the radio and television networks for the opportunities they have given me over the years to bring reports and messages to our nation. My special thanks go to them for the opportunity of addressing you this evening.

Three days from now, after half a century in the service of our country, I shall lay down the responsibilities of office as, in traditional and solemn ceremony, the authority of the Presidency is vested in my successor.

This evening I come to you with a message of leave-taking and farewell, and to share a few final thoughts with you, my countrymen.

Like every other citizen, I wish the new President, and all who will labor with him, Godspeed. I pray that the coming years will be blessed with peace and prosperity for all.

93

Our people expect their President and the Congress to find essential agreement on issues of great moment, and wise resolution of which will better shape the future of the nation.

My own relations with the Congress, which began on a remote and tenuous basis when, long ago, a member of the Senate appointed me to West Point, have since ranged to the intimate during the war and immediate postwar period, and finally to the mutually interdependent during these past eight years.

In this final relationship, the Congress and the Administration have, on most vital issues, cooperated well, to serve the nation good rather than mere partisanship, and so have assured that the business of the nation should go forward. So my official relationship with the Congress ends in a feeling on my part, of gratitude that we have been able to do so much together.

We now stand ten years past the midpoint of a century that has witnessed four major wars among great nations—three of these involved our own country.

Despite these holocausts America is today the strongest, the most influential and most productive nation in the world. Understandably proud of this preeminence, we yet realize that America's leadership and prestige depend, not merely upon our unmatched material progress, riches and military strength, but on how we use our power in the interests of world peace and human betterment.

Throughout America's adventure in free government, our basic purposes have been to keep the peace; to foster progress in human achievement, and to enhance liberty, dignity, and integrity among peoples and among nations.

To strive for less would be unworthy of a free and religious people.

Any failure traceable to arrogance or our lack of comprehension or readiness to sacrifice would inflict upon us grievous hurt, both at home and abroad.

Progress toward these noble goals is persistently threatened by the conflict now engulfing the world. It commands our whole attention, absorbs our very beings.

We face a hostile ideology—global in scope, atheistic in character, ruthless in purpose and insidious in method. Unhappily the danger it poses promises to be of indefinite duration. To meet it successfully there is called for, not so much the emotional transitory sacrifices of crisis, but rather those which enable us to carry forward steadily, surely and without complaint the burdens of a prolonged and complex struggle—with liberty at stake.

Only thus shall we remain, despite every provocation, on our chartered course toward permanent peace and human betterment.

Crises there will continue to be. In meeting them, whether foreign or domestic, great or small, there is a recurring temptation to feel that some spectacular and costly action could become the miraculous solution to all current difficulties. A huge increase in newer elements of our defenses; development of unrealistic programs to cure every ill in agriculture; a dramatic expansion in basic and applied research—these and many other possibilities, each possibly promising in itself, may be suggested as the only way to the road we wish to travel.

But each proposal must be weighed in the light of a broader consideration; the need to maintain balance in and among national programs—balance between the private and the public economy, balance between the cost and hoped for advantages—balance between the clearly necessary and the comfortably desirable; balance between our essential requirements as a nation and the duties imposed by the nation upon the individual; balance between actions of the moment and the national welfare of the future. Good judgment seeks balance and progress; lack of it eventually finds imbalance and frustration.

The record of many decades stands as proof that our people and their Government have, in the main, understood these truths and have responded to them well in the face of threat and stress.

But threats, new in kind or degree, constantly arise. Of these, I mention two only.

A vital element in keeping the peace is our military establishment. Our arms must be mighty, ready for instant action, so that no potential aggressor may be tempted to risk his own destruction.

Our military organization today bears little relation to that known of any of my predecessors in peacetime —or, indeed, by the fighting men of World War II or Korea.

Until the latest of our world conflicts, the United States had no armaments industry. American makers of plowshares could, with time and as required, make swords as well.

But we can no longer risk emergency improvisation of national defense. We have been compelled to create a permanent armaments industry of vast proportions. Added to this, three and a half million men and women are directly engaged in the defense establishment. We annually spend on military security alone more than the net income of all United States corporations.

Now this conjunction of an immense military establishment and a large arms industry is new in the American experience. The total influence—economic, political, even spiritual—is felt in every city, every state house, every office of the Federal Government. We recognize the imperative need for this development. Yet we must not fail to comprehend its grave implications. Our toil, resources, and livelihood are all involved; so is the very structure of our society.

In the councils of Government, we must guard against the acquisition of unwarranted influence, whether sought or unsought, by the military-industrial complex. The potential for the disastrous rise of misplaced power exists and will persist.

We must never let the weight of this combination endanger our liberties or democratic processes. We should take nothing for granted. Only an alert and knowledgeable citizenry can compel the proper meshing of the huge industrial and military machinery of defense with our peaceful methods and goals, so that security and liberty may prosper together.

Akin to, and largely responsible for the sweeping changes in our industrial-military posture has been the technological revolution during recent decades.

In this revolution research has become central. It

also becomes more formalized, complex, and costly. A steadily increasing share is conducted for, by, or at the direction of the Federal Government.

Today the solitary inventor, tinkering in his shop, has been overshadowed by task forces of scientists, in laboratories and testing fields. In the same fashion, the free university, historically the fountainhead of free ideas and scientific discovery, has experienced a revolution in the conduct of research. Partly because of the huge costs involved, a Government contract becomes virtually a substitute for intellectual curiosity.

For every old blackboard there are now hundreds of new electronic computers.

The prospect of domination of the nation's scholars by Federal employment, project allocations, and the power of money is ever present, and is gravely to be regarded.

Yet, in holding scientific research and discovery in respect, as we should, we must also be alert to the equal and opposite danger that public policy could itself become the captive of a scientific-technological elite.

It is the task of statesmanship to mold, to balance, and to integrate these and other forces, new and old, within the principles of our democratic system—ever aiming toward the supreme goals of our free society.

Another factor in maintaining balance involves the element of time. As we peer into society's future, we—you and I, and our Government—must avoid the impulse to live only for today, plundering, for our own ease and convenience, the precious resources of tomorrow.

We cannot mortgage the material assets of our grandchildren without risking the loss also of their political and spiritual heritage. We want democracy to survive for all generations to come, not to become the insolvent phantom of tomorrow.

During the long lane of the history yet to be written America knows that this world of ours, ever growing smaller, must avoid becoming a community of dreadful fear and hate, and be, instead, a proud confederation of mutual trust and respect.

Such a confederation must be one of equals. The weakest must come to the conference table with the same confidence as do we, protected as we are by our moral, economic, and military strength. That table, though scarred by many past frustrations, cannot be abandoned for the certain agony of the battlefield.

Disarmament, with mutual honor and confidence, is a continuing imperative. Together, we must learn how to compose differences—not with arms, but with intellect and decent purpose. Because this need is so sharp and apparent, I confess that I lay down my official responsibilities in this field with a definite sense of disappointment. As one who has witnessed the horror and the lingering sadness of war, as one who knows that another war could utterly destroy this civilization which has been so slowly and painfully built over thousands of years, I wish I could say tonight that a lasting peace is in sight.

Happily, I can say that war has been avoided. Steady progress toward our ultimate goal has been made. But so much remains to be done. As a private citizen, I shall never cease to do what little I can to help the world advance along that road.

So, in this, my last good night to you as your President, I thank you for the many opportunities you have given me for public service in war and in peace.

I trust that, in that service, you find some things worthy. As for the rest of it, I know you will find ways to improve performance in the future.

You and I—my fellow citizens—need to be strong in our faith that all nations, under God, will reach the goal of peace with justice. May we be ever unswerving in devotion to principle, confident but humble with power, diligent in pursuit of the nation's great goals.

To all the peoples of the world, I once more give expression to America's prayerful and continuing aspiration:

We pray that peoples of all faiths, all races, all nations, may have their great human needs satisfied; that those now denied opportunity shall come to enjoy it to the full; that all who yearn for freedom may experience its spiritual blessings, those who have freedom will understand, also, its heavy responsibility; that all who are insensitive to the needs of others, will learn charity, and that the scourges of poverty, disease, and ignorance will be made to disappear from the earth and that in the goodness of time, all peoples will come to live together in a peace guaranteed by the binding force of mutual respect and love.

Now, on Friday noon, I am to become a private citizen. I am proud to do so. I look forward to it.

Thank you, and good night.